DON'T IDENTIFY WITH IT
BEGINNING THE PHILOSOPHICAL JOURNEY TOWARD SELF-EMPOWERMENT

H. T. Waters

Copyright © 2023 by H. T. Waters
All rights reserved. No part of this book may be reproduced or used in any manner without written permission of the copyright owner except for the use of quotations in a book review. For more information, contact address: HT@HTwaters.com
First e-book edition June 2023
Online version published June 2023
Cover Image Copyright pending 2023
Book Design: H. T. Waters
Editorial Services provided by Marsha Phillips
ISBN: 979-8-9884572-1-3 (e-book)
ISBN: 979-8-9884572-2-0 (paperback)

HTWaters.com

I dedicate this book to all the lost souls who know there is more to this world and can see the potential of all things—and no-thing.

DON'T IDENTIFY WITH IT

And so...my soul begins with a question and ends with a quote...
-H.T. Waters

Contents

Introduction

Chapter 1. Why Identity Matters (Don't Follow the Rules When It Means Dying)

Chapter 2. Buddhism and a New Self-Concept

Chapter 3. How Past Philosophers Help Us Break Free of Dogma

Chapter 4. Deception as Identity or Agenda

Chapter 5. The "T'ude" Limitation

Chapter 6. There Is "No Place like Earth"

Chapter 7. Self-Empowerment Creates Empowerment for Others

Chapter 8. If We Have Nothing Left to Believe, What Do We Believe?

Chapter 9. The Matrix and the Blue Pill

Chapter 10. Opinions—Everyone Has One

Chapter 11. We Are All Criminally Insane

Chapter 12. It's Not Kansas, but It's a Potential

Introduction

Philosophy creates a maze of interconnecting tunnels that dumbfounds the cleverest rabbit. It is often inaccessible due to the philosopher's tendency to "think things to death," which inevitably collides with practical survival. Why should one care about the musings of Kant or Nietzsche when shelter, food, and comfort must be consistently sought or secured, or when one is facing the harsh realities of war, crime, and pandemics? In short: "Why should I care about philosophy, when I have to work, pay bills, and hustle to survive?" The reason is, we cannot (nor should we) return to a place where respect for knowledge—the search for truth—no longer inspires us.

From the Buddhist temple to the histrionics of politics, someone is constantly telling us how and what to think so we may become better—or worst, so we may follow blindly; after all, Hitler had a philosophy. From vaccination to fair election deniers, we live in a time where truth is subjective even when science says otherwise; "fear becomes friend" because we believe it keeps us safe from those who will manipulate the system on a grand scale. For example, in 2020, Donald Trump was able to sway masses of people by telling them the November election was stolen, even after 60 courts said differently. An individual's truth and universal truth are not the same. Universal truths, like mathematical equations, always have the same provable outcome; i.e., $2+2=4$, similar to some scientific conclusions, such as the benefits of vaccinations outweighing the risk of not getting them. To eliminate fear, we must understand ourselves so we are not easily fooled by snake oil salesmen or destructive politicians.

Philosophy fails when it comes to uncertainty and fear (and academic virtue, where the noble erudite—unemployed—mumble in isolation). Though philosophy can potentially lead to a fascination with dystopia—a nihilistic approach to our reality—it can also, as a tool, free the mind and help us navigate questions about life, death, and purpose. Philosophy is around us, always, and can and should be an anchor for our lost ship—our humanity. If you understand yourself, your weaknesses, your chosen identities, if you know how you think and respond, then you cannot be a pawn to your ego or other people. We have the power to choose who we are and what we do with our lives, and to choose well. It is possible to live in a state of mindful liberty;[1] still, it must be considered that our social contract is integral to survival. Though some of us prefer solitude and can survive alone, most see and need others as anchors. There is a good balance between needing community and being able to think for ourselves—stripped of belief systems that may harm us or others. Philosophy's value resides in its ability to help us rethink dogma, for when we question everything, beliefs—like leaves—shed; or they become stronger, their roots resting deep in the earth. For example, at times, philosophical books provide "thought puzzles" that often revolve around how many people die in a brawl or by a trolly, presenting a choice that can change based on presented facts, typically like this:

> You are driving a trolley whose brakes have failed.
>
> You can only turn right or left.
>
> On the right, there is a recently released prisoner who has done dastardly deeds throughout her life; on the left, there is a baby in a stroller.
>
> You will hit one of these people. *Which do you save?* (Or, *which do you kill?*)

You would probably choose to hit the released prisoner. However, we learn that the ex-prisoner had been arrested because she is a freedom fighter working to free people from oppression, and at times, certain death, and plans to continue doing so. Now the thought puzzle switches to *baby vs. freedom fighter*. You may still decide to hit the

DON'T IDENTIFY WITH IT

freedom fighter and spare the baby. However, this time, the freedom fighter is replaced by three brain surgeons. Now the choice is *baby vs. three surgeons*. The idea is that the more facts change, opinions about who to save changes, based on what the observer values and the number of persons in question.

Such thought puzzles can leave one lost in a dystopian society where the richest, smartest, and most privileged survive. However, they also help us to be creative with our thinking. The box is no longer where the mind and ideas reside and we are less swayed by what others think when we question everything.

In this book, I pose emotionally triggering ideas to help you think about your beliefs and how those beliefs might impact others. Making people rethink, reevaluate, and remake themselves is my goal. Your being uncomfortable means that I am making inroads to your identity construct. If you feel discomfort, this means there is something in you that recognizes the truth of what I say. We all need to be more uncomfortable. Whether you disagree with me on any point, or if you agree, contemplate your conclusion; after all, this is not about me and my beliefs, but for you to think beyond the obvious, *to think for yourself*. My goal is to provide tools to help you expand your identity so you can function and act positively in an often-chaotic world. I offer ideas, through philosophical questioning, about how you may approach everyday living. I, however, would not and will not tell you what to believe; that is something you must discover for yourself.

Another important point of interest is the issue of mental health, which has become a substantial problem in the U.S., especially for youth,[2] including (but not excluding) chemical imbalances, the harshness of poverty, lack of opportunity, and low self-worth. Can philosophical inquiry help with mental health? Potentially—for it offers tools to help change how a person identifies with ideas that keep them stuck. In this book, I cut to the chase. I give you tools to help improve your mental abilities through intuition, ancient philosophical reasoning, and practical application—not as a replacement for mental health professionals or academia, but as a supplement or anchor. We will work to reach your core and, from there, expand mentally, intuitively, and spiritually. One major issue in today's society is not knowing who we truly are individually and collectively; how to navigate different cultures, ideas, and possibilities without being swayed by others' agendas, themes, or lies. We need to bring back a human identity that focuses on self-empowerment, creativity, and empathy. Each person must look within to see where their fundamental beliefs come from and where we differ in finding common ground. What tools will we use? Philosophical discourse, questioning, and intuition.

Philosophy and philosophers must bring forth ideas easily understood and not merely for academic masturbation. Unlike the spiritualist or scientist, philosophers gain knowledge through the systematic questioning of things that cannot be answered by intuition or methodology alone. Philosophy relies on a combination of both. Some hardcore philosophers would disagree with me and say that intuition has no part in philosophy. But, just like Archimedes came to his *Eureka!* moment in the bathtub, intuition plays an integral part in observation, in how it plays out through experience, and the *ah-ha* moments we may experience every day. I propose to make philosophy accessible and useful.

Chapter 1
Why Identity Matters (Don't Follow the Rules When It Means Dying)

Fiona didn't understand why she wasn't good enough; she had dressed right—in her white stilettos and tight black dress. Others were watching, she knew. She looked back at the crowd glaring at her with disdain, impatience—even pity. The lights from the Club Vibe sign bounced across the damp sidewalk, evidence of an early spring. Fiona's eyes roved up the bouncer's black t-shirt. A military type, he stood arms crossed and unmoved. She flinched as he looked down at her through black sunglasses. "Miss, we can't let you in. You aren't on the list."

Only the demographically rich and connected got through the doors, those who didn't meet those criteria served as eye-candy.

The bouncer pulled out a card, handed it to Fiona, and waved his tattooed arm toward an alley that appeared to smell slightly of vomit and cat piss. "Step over there."

Fiona looked at the card. On it were words she could not quite work out. The bouncer, seeing her squint, pointed across the cobblestone street, where an obscure sign jutted out from the wall at a right angle. "Go there, you won't regret it," he lisped—a fairly genuine gesture from a man responsible for human aesthetic segregation; a modern Nazi in a disparate world of influencers, TikTokers, and haters.

Fiona took a step off the curb, turned one more time, and sighed. She heard the bouncer mumble something and noticed another aesthetically displeasing couple being turned away. Interestingly enough, the bouncer didn't give them a card. Fiona's shoes made a distinctive hollow tap-tap as she carefully tip-toed across the cobblestones in the alley. Somehow, the pressure of the card in her hand gave comfort, a sort of existential handshake. As she stopped under the sign, a titanic doom came over her. The first words were:

The Bloodied Soul's

...and in small letters beneath them:

Refuge

"The Bloodied Soul's Refuge." The name sounded like a hipster dump for the alienated communist—too intellectual—but she had nowhere else to go. Fiona approached the iron door—black; heavy. She pushed the door open, easily.

Fiona vaguely remembered a Groucho Marx quote: "I'd never join a club that would have me as a member"...or something like that. As she opened the door, Fiona was blasted with pulsating asynchronistic music. The door closed with a thud. The back of the door was embellished with a velvet red, pillow-like fabric, camouflaged by a wall of similar material. This was definitely not a political club—although maybe a conservative one.

Inside, small wooden tables were surrounded by two or three customers—some were headless! Fiona raised her hand to her mouth to suppress a scream, and possibly vomit, but as her eyes adjusted to the dim light, she found these weren't people at all, but mannequins.

She looked back at the door, but decided not to try it for fear she would find she was locked in. Red velvet was everywhere—on the seats, around the centered stage, and the curtains along the walls—a gothic romantic drama. To the right, Fiona saw an electronic box with words scrolling across its face—like in a financial building, reporting stocks—only these were words:

People ... are ... Hell.

The words would pause in full sentence, then flash. She recognized the quote from her Philosophy 101 course. On the lefthand side was another rectangular box hanging from the ceiling:

As soon as ... you have a thought ... laugh at it.

Maybe she could google the quote and take pictures for later. Fiona reached inside her black sequined handbag for her phone. It wasn't there! A bit of bile rose in her throat... "Calm down Fiona," she said aloud, "remember, you left your phone at home because it was broken."

"You left home without your phone?" said a voice from somewhere.

Fiona looked up, then she looked down, and there he was ... a small person.

"Yeah. I'm a dwarf and you're fat. Let's get over it."

She realized she'd been staring, but the fat remark stung (too many times rejected, overlooked, pitied). She pulled her eyes away and mumbled, "What is this place?"

"I don't know. I thought you'd tell me. But it looks like we're in this together, whatever it is..." He pointed a stumpy finger toward the door. "It's locked. We can't get out."

Fiona felt laughter welling up inside her. Was this some sort of performance art? A bar joke? Something like, "A fat girl, a dwarf, and a rabbi walk into the bar..." She grinned.

"What are you laughing at?" The man looked up at her, furious or curious, she couldn't tell.

"Oh, sorry. I don't know your name."

"Jack."

"I'm Fiona... I just had an absurd thought. We are in someone's performance art piece, the stars of the show. Someone is watching us flounder about." She imitated a person falling, her hand swinging the golden chain of her purse like a soft pendulum counting down minutes.

Jack grunted, "I'm stuck in this room with some crazy-ass white chick who thinks she's a diva..."

"*Lady and Gentleman.*" *A feminine, automated voice sounded from the speakers nestled in the corners of the octagon room.* "*Please take your seats.*" *Fiona hadn't noticed the musical overture now filling the room, one familiar to ... she wasn't sure ... a Broadway musical?*

There was a loud clunk and the overhead lights went out. Two spotlights shined on two chairs onstage.

Neither Jack nor Fiona moved. They looked at each other. Jack pointed at a seat. Fiona shook her head. The monotoned voice came again. "*Please take your seats.*" *The two waited.*

Fiona knew there would be an impasse if no one sat, that nothing would happen. She wasn't sure why she did it, but she felt an urge to remove her shoes. Her fingers shook as she freed her ankles from the straps. Her shoes dangled from her fingers as she walked, slowly, toward the spotlights, toward the chairs—wooden and lonely.

She sat.

Turn left... Turn left... My phone spoke in an attractive lilting female voice, with a foreign accent. I looked to my left: there was the empty carpool lane and a freeway barrier—white solid—though only about one foot wide, not jumpable in a large burgundy SUV. *Redirecting... Redirecting...* I glanced at my phone to see where the navigation app was leading me and contemplated whether I could take Google to court for the resulting mayhem I would face if I did take a left turn or... *Turn Right... Turn Right...* My phone continued to insist on creating severe auto impaction and certain death. I imagined people screaming and cursing the idiotic female driver. I gripped the steering wheel and wondered why engineers keep making our lives more complicated. *Turn Right....* At that point, the lovely voice screamed at me again (probably able to tell I wasn't listening). I looked right. There were three lanes of traffic moving approximately 5 mph in a 65-mph zone, which, on a Silicon Valley freeway, isn't bad for 8:30a.m. on a Monday morning; however, turning right was decidedly dangerous. It's the law in California that, while driving, you cannot pick up your phone to turn it off, nor can you turn right, across, and perpendicular to the on-coming traffic…I was stuck.

What do I do when I am stuck? I practice mindfulness. With the phone still in my ear speaking commands of a dangerous sort, I entered my zone. I kept driving straight; I did not turn right or left.

I thought about "god," as in "technology," and how we seem to live our lives with faith in it, belying common sense. As a non-engineer, do I have the right to criticize the Silicon Valley reality of our freeway system? A navigational system that would have you turn *right* into on-coming traffic over and over, while driving on a major highway?

Today's technology has permeated our lives; in some cases, to the determinant of spiritual and ethical realities. I somewhat view technology as a hubris, much like those who raged about the invincibility of the Titanic, which on its first voyage *sank*. There is a blind faith in something people believe will solve the world's problems; yet, if it continues along its current course, will we eventually sink? My I-phone once only required a finger touch to open—the biometrics feature was helpful—but now? The fingerprint feature on my I-phone 8 doesn't work since the 300th Apple upgrade. Today, instead of doctors playing god, we have thousands of omnipresent tech gurus believing they have the answer to our problems. If they are going to take jobs from thousands of people (including cartographers) with "efficiency" upgrades, the devices should at least work.

So why has technology started to fail as time goes on? Why take a well-functioning app and "upgrade" it to the point where it potentially guides users into on-coming traffic? Technology fails over time because high-tech companies do not see through the eyes of the user. They work for the betterment of their bottom line through more upgrades and planned obsolescence—nothing lasts, which means more money spent by users. Technology has taken over most of the world, making its creators money. Even the housing crisis in Silicon Valley has meant people who provide essential services in the Bay Area (teachers, police officers, and firefighters) cannot afford to live there.

See technology for its uses, but do not let it replace your ability to reason. It is obvious that turning at a 90°angle into parallel traffic is a bad idea, but there are times when navigating our personal world will not be so straightforward, but requires that we follow our own ideals, not imposed rules. Our ideals stem from our identity. Our identity is what makes us who we are and it is constantly changing, if we allow it. I say "allow" because it is easy to become set in a particular story or narrative concerning our identity. In fact, the "narrative" that identity exists is a subset of the philosophical idea of "notions of self."

If we are set in our identity, we are also potentially dogmatic, and if we are dogmatic, our opinions are no longer just opinions but expressions of a deep-seated belief system that can potentially manipulate us. It is imperative to build a core identity that will help us navigate life, allowing us to not only deal with the world but *act* in the world. To do this, we must challenge our first constructs: who we really are and where "I" resides. Here is a short meditative exercise:

> Close your eyes. Place your thumb and forefinger together.
>
> What do you feel in your thumb? In your forefinger? Nerve endings tingling? Focus on this sensation.
>
> Do not think.
>
> Breathe.
>
> Find the silence between the breath.
>
> Now ask yourself, *who* is this?
>
> Some might receive an answer from an inner voice. Try releasing this expectation.

DON'T IDENTIFY WITH IT

Focus in-between breaths again, to a point where there are no thoughts, no voices in your head.

When I first did this, I was frightened. The space between breaths can be deafening, or a cliff where you are suspended with one foot on its edge, the other in the air. In spirituality, it is called *the void*. It is used to indicate where salvation and truth can be found. [3] [4] This silence is the place from which we can begin. Go to the silent place of non-identification, non-judgment, and non-permanence and you will start to see the world, *everything*, differently. Some experience spiritual awakening in this space. What the sacred provides in this silence is the ability to touch consciousness, but not be attached to outcomes. This is where we start to become more of who we are and release preconceived ideas of who we should be.[5] This takes courage and commitment. This is where the identity journey begins without navigation, without direction. This silent place will allow you to create your own identity, and it provides a road map.

Chapter 2
Buddhism and a New Self-Concept

Buddhism offers a practical philosophy on how to build a new self-concept: start within the void. To embark on the journey to a new identity without a faulty navigational system, consider the concept of "non-self," as opposed to "no-self," which implies a non-functioning person. Non-self implies not identifying with the material, thereby allowing significant internal and external changes.[6] Buddhists do not follow the intellectual interpretation of non-self; they believe a person needs to practice in order to fully understand its meaning.

Let us explore why Buddhism extracts the self from everyday material existence. Foremost is the idea of non-permanence. If we have a self, we are attached to a specific reality, and since change is constant, if we grasp at permanence, we are bound to suffer. In short, we all die; so, if we are attached to our identity, the mere thought triggers an egoic response to annihilation: fear. Only by relinquishing attachment to self can we truly be free from suffering. It is the same with the body. Identifying with the body cannot be a constant because we all age and experience other physical changes; hence, Locke came up with the idea of the constant consciousness to anchor the identity with an attribute determined by memory.[7] Your memories, false or not, create your identity. However, this becomes problematic because many people do not remember specifics in their life. Memories are lost, so their identity cannot be constant. Additionally, people do not remember their birth, and according to Locke's view, your first memory creates your identity. Now, if you put Buddhism in such a scenario, memory does not matter. We are not "selves," hence memory is not required for us to exist in the material world. If we become attached to the body, we become reminded of physical death. We all die, we are all subject to the decay of life, but if you accept the non-permanence of life, the self becomes a non-issue.

There are five aggregates, or skandhas, and within this is an aggregate of senses, not unlike Hume's.[8] In reality, experiences are not our identity; however, reality is experience. We smell, hear, think, touch, taste, but this is the whole of reality—our experiences. Modern science pushes material things, but the physical world is just experiences and our interpretation of them.

As you move through the day, everything changes; sights and sounds come and go. Change is easy for the non-self because there is no need for a constant identity; there is no solid foundation of "I." As you continue to watch the changing world, it appears to be a superficial existence. Buddhism expounds that to have a full understanding of life, one must train the mind. Meditation creates a sense of peace; suffering and thinking fall away once you are simply breath. Because things that fade are not your identity, they cannot be who you are. This is the path to non-suffering and happiness. Once you get to the stripped-down version of "you" through practice, you leave attachment behind. You embody a sense of freedom, peace, and happiness. All things in the world are not yours, you are not permanent, you can only allow things to be. There is no control, just "allowing" and nonattachment, so you do not need to be attached to wanting and yearning as the material world is an illusion.

Mark Siderits' paper, "Buddhist Non-Self: The No-Owner's Manual," discusses how the narrative framework of self offers the Buddhist the presence needed to have memories for a personhood on earth, but only to a certain point. How can suffering exist without a self to be conscious of pain? You cannot recognize the existence of suffering without feeling, experiencing, or seeing it yourself. At that point, you can release attachment to suffering and self to become enlightened. The material world provides learning tools to see the world and become knowledgeable of how to release attachments.

Moral Obligations and the Non-Self

If the fundamental problem with a non-self is the perpetual nebulous, why should I care about anyone? If others have no self-identity to protect, I owe nothing to the individual. A new social contract must then exist. The human community would need to create additional guidelines; i.e., if we give up the self and do not see self in each other, we then need to focus on the collective good. At first glance, this may seem marginally positive, for we are now thinking about the greater good in a utilitarian way. This, however, becomes problematic if the collective has gone down a dark path of human sacrifice for the sake of dogma. Consider if, at the beginning, each of us is thinking of a heaven above where we need to secure a place through a human or animal sacrifice or community ritual and this ends up being a bloodbath to appease the gods. No one would be waving their arms saying, "I will not be sacrificed because I have an identity worth preserving." However, Buddhism believes this is a superficial interpretation of non-self as it pre-supposes no moral obligation.

If we believe in impermanence and there is a non-self, we are less likely to try "saving" ourselves or seeking a moral superiority over others; hence, a life of self-reflection could follow as we would not chase the perpetual tail of trying to "better" a self if it does not exist—nor would we compare ourselves, so we would not need to be materially embroiled in the rat race. If there is no self, there is no reason to preserve the ego, the part of us that demands survival. Death has no meaning without self; there is no fear of impermanence—we are mere players in a game of life, free to be more altruistic because it makes us feel good.

Buddhism Answers to a Nihilistic Approach to Self

A concept of a non-self that removes attachment to the material conceptually annihilates any need to care about the world. *Why bother if there is nothing to work for concerning self-identification? I am not looking to improve myself because my ego no longer needs anything; I am only here to experience, but not be attached. So, ultimately, why should I* care? Why not just meditate alone and seek nirvana without interactions? Why care about anything if everything is suffering and if to release suffering I need only release myself from attachments? Buddhism would say the "we" is more important than the "I." (Alone or in groups, Buddhist monks reach nirvana, a state of non-self in the universe.) A Buddhist would likely say non-self is about releasing the need to identify with the physical, but that does not mean we should not experience it. We are a conglomerate of senses: our world is experienced so we can understand suffering and physicality. The intellectualism of non-self without Buddhist practices lends itself to a superficial understanding; hence, a Buddhist encourages practical application.

Focusing on a non-self potentially means being more cognizant of "others" and being less individuated. Buddhism provides purposeful recognition where the emptiness of non-identification could lead to disastrous results of potential non-recognition of self in others by creating a collective. A Buddhist greeting, *Anjali Mudra*, is hands together in a bow, combined with a greeting in the other person's language, e.g., "Welcome" in English or "Namaste" in Hindi. The use of differing languages in a Buddhist tradition means the individual meets the collective. The empathetic recognition of "others" means Buddhism is not looking to replace the self with nothing, but places it firmly in the hands of the collective recognition of "otherness."

The response of Buddhist tenets to our individualistic tendencies in Western traditions is valuable: not seeing the self as existing in self-identification, in order to prevent suffering, provides a gateway to relearning empathy and a more inclusive thought process. It ultimately releases the need for a continuity of identity, which troubles many philosophers, as memories are lost, physical characteristics change, moral values morph, and our sense of who we are no longer matters in a physical sense.

Chapter 3
How Past Philosophers Help Us Break Free of Dogma

"The death of dogma is the birth of morality." – Immanual Kant

"It is better to change an opinion than persist in a wrong one." – Socrates

I am an unapologetic feminist; yet, I believe in the analytical feminist tradition where we can learn from philosophical traditions of dead male philosophers; I will leverage their ideas throughout this work. That said, I think it is important for us to delve outside our comfort zones, so we do not get stuck identifying with dogma. There is a difference between dogma and opinion, as pointed out by the two quotations above. Dogma is seen as a set of rules often based on opinions (i.e., politics) or myth (i.e., religion), which cannot be challenged by the believer. Opinions, on the other hand, can and should be challenged. The problem is, today people are unwilling to change their opinions.

Socrates' Method

Socrates believed that no one has the *only* opinion, only that some opinions are closer to the truth; hence, he wanted truth-finding to be the basis of a discussion. In his teaching methodology, he continued to question his students until he was able to determine that there was a sound conclusion or method to the argument. This methodology became known as the *Socratic method*, which is still used in law school to help budding students aspire to manipulation and/or truth seeking.

Statement (S): "This is an apple."

Socratic Method (SM): "How do you know it's an apple?"

S: "Its color."

SM: "What is the color?"

S: "Red."

SM: "Aren't there other things that are red?"

S: "Yes."

SM: "So, why is this apple's red different from the red of the kerchief you are wearing?"

The Socratic method of questioning enables people to break down where they may be emotionally charged within a system of beliefs. When we are emotionally charged by a belief system, we are often wrongly attached. I use the word "wrongly" because truth does not have to be a nebulous, unattainable abstract, but a rational relationship between science and experience, hence why the deductive reasoning process is so important. Cue Aristotle.

Aristotle and Deductive Reasoning

Deductive reasoning does not need to be hard, but it is invaluable when discussing someone's belief system(s) and helps us become more humane in general. An example of a faulty deductive reasoning paradigm is the following:

Adam ate an apple Eve gave him.

Adam decided he didn't like being naked.

Eve was evil.

Now, if Adam ate an apple, we can believe this to be a valid premise, however, what we do not know from these statements is if eating the apple was the reason Adam did not like being naked. Also, the third statement, that Eve was evil, has no logical connection between any of these statements. These statements are not valid and are not subject to a test on validity. This is not to be confused with research validity, which has to do with scientific method and experimentation.

Religion as Mythology

Regarding the story of Adam and Eve, it is impossible to believe it is anything but myth. There is no evidence to back up the premises. Taking "deductive reasoning" out of just premises and conclusion, and including substantial evidence or experiences, is important. Then you get to the nitty gritty of reality; i.e., can you figure out if the evidence is false? You can use research validity by doing experiments and using experience to determine factual premises. The book of Genesis has no factual references, no evidence of a tree, talking snake, and no footnotes; in truth, no facts to back it up. It is a myth that has meaning to theologians, but to the rest of us, it is a story about how sin was leveraged to make women feel "less than," as the story and "rib" reference are marginalizing.

Let's switch it around. Let's say God was only talking to Eve. God told Eve that he was going to give her a companion because she seemed lonely and paradise was wearing on her, so she agreed. He took her rib and made another person, Adam, who was also naked. Adam, being bored and hungry, went and talked to the snake though God and Eve had told him over and over again not to, but he didn't listen. He took the apple, bit it, and then they had to be fully clothed and banished from paradise. Once you shift the paradigm from a female causing problems to a man causing problems you start to see where we have gone wrong. If you are a man, how does this make you feel when you read this story about Eve being the one in power? What if you came from a woman's rib? What if you had tempted Eve instead? Re-write the story from another's perspective and you can empathize more with their plight.

Who wrote the story of Adam and Eve first? The people with power in those days: men. They explained how things were set up so they could support their specific agenda. Everyone has an agenda, what suits their particular belief system. If you believe in power over others, you will want your narrative to suit that need and will tell yourself lies, myths, and facts to support it. It may be unconscious, but it is still an agenda. Agendas are not necessarily bad—they just underlie who we are at a core level and can impact our actions. Consider Mother Teresa's agenda to bring more people into her Catholic faith.[9] Religion is one of the greatest proponents of blind faith, but issues arise when the blind lead the blind. Faith is a deeply held belief and makes us, as humans, do foolish things because we want to fit in, or we were told to follow orders, or we are a prophet of sorts. We can release ourselves from the dogma of our agendas if we delve deeper. I also have an agenda, yet I am not "anti-religion" but a strong believer that everyone has a right to practice their religion as long as others are not forced to conform and are not harmed because of those beliefs. It is important to understand the agenda factor for your own self-growth and be wary of things people tell you.

If we believe everyone has an agenda, how do we rethink our identity? Agendas form identities by creating stories and beliefs that support what we need to survive. Whether perceived or survival-based, they are fundamentally the same. Our real job is to figure out our agendas by knowing our triggers. If it's religion, we'll be triggered by people who make fun of our god, goddess, or what we were told by others to believe. Demystifying our agenda is important for authenticity and being able to respond mindfully to our environment. If we do not understand the truth of our reality through our perceived belief system and the potential biases this creates, we are not able to deconstruct misinformation.

If you are a religious person, did my reference to "myths" upset you viscerally? You might not have felt anything. Though you are religious, you might see the idea of myth as valid because the Bible is full of stories; you might not believe Moses parted the Red Sea. Alternatively, you might have gotten upset because my "story," within the premises, is not true to the Bible, which I would grant you as I do not purport to be a religious scholar, I am just making a point. Yet, if you are set in your religion, you can see it as being the full narrative of who you are. It is what you identify with, what you have placed your faith in, and how you deal with the world. Your belief in your god and the beliefs around the establishment of that god, allows you a community—a group who can help you function and there are rules to follow. Fundamentally, you are unwilling to change your opinion because you are emotionally attached to the idea of having stability in your life. Religion provides an anchor for that; yet, I am asking you to challenge it. The reason to challenge any belief system is to be able to sift through what is viable and what is potentially dangerous. People twist the world around them to fit their agenda, whether it be men saying women are property so they can control them, or a whole group of people are seen as not human so they cannot have the same rights as they do—these are dangerous dogmas. On the other hand, Christianity has some good beliefs: help one's neighbor; judge not, lest you be judged; treat others the way you would want to be treated—these are virtues that strive to uplift, include, and empathize.

It is important to have tools to see where we need to deconstruct agendas tied to belief systems. It's one thing to call someone's beliefs moronic, but unless we can walk them through *why* they have swerved from the truth, there will be no path *to* the truth.

It's even harder to find the unconscious agenda because this might be based on a person's background. Colonialists were famous for their agendas based on their biases of manifest destiny birthed from white superiority. They had to create an agenda from their superior identity in order to dominate. What better than to make it "God's will"? No matter where someone's personal beliefs come from, if you believe you are superior to anyone, you are on a road to seeking power over others or things, and need to create an agenda and identity that suits your desire for domination. If superiority is part of your identity, you are a danger to others.

Today, right-wing radicals also embrace these ideas of superiority which, more likely than not, come from a long line of religious indoctrination based on damnation and fear (fear of being replaced and their voices being marginalized because they are no longer the majority). Now, as a progressive nation, our biases tend to see hatred, anger, and marginalization in everything. We are easily offended when someone wears braids a certain way because this is considered cultural appropriation. Being offended is a sure sign of a trigger and you should look deep into whether or not the trigger comes from an agenda and belief system that is part of your shadow self, or if it is deeply rooted in a need for justice. Taking offense is a way to marginalize your own voice—don't do it. Taking offense is not about justice, it is about a personal belief and agenda, whereby you see yourself as being attacked and as a victim. It becomes all about *you*. One benefit of stripping down your identity is becoming able to see and look at what might be triggering you. If you can continue to come from the point of emptiness and silence, you can observe your life, your personality, character, beliefs, and body. You may start to notice that your beliefs create shadow aspects.

Philosophers delve into ethics; that which separates, degrades, negates, and oppresses on the ethics spectrum would be considered destructive ethics, ethics which would not hold up to Aristotle's virtuous life theory. How do we find the virtuous life? By working through belief systems that hold us separate and oppressed, via others or ourselves. I challenge you to see if you can find your trigger point of separation, as you may well find it within your own consciousness. For example, whether your desire for wealth comes from survival or a place of superiority, the belief system you bring to wealth is what decides your ethics. If you want to eat and believe the only way you can eat is to take from others, you are creating a separation within yourself of the "have and have nots" instead of seeing the world as providing for everyone. At the point where you understand your connection with others, you stop seeing separateness, and are more likely to see them as part of humanity. If you see anyone with lack, you are more likely to provide for them or others as this brings you together as a part of humanity. Once you focus on the connection between us, the more likely you will attempt to reach out, see people for who they are, and take a moment to provide comfort or *be* comforted by another. Judgment of, and separation from, others breeds superiority, elitism, and de-humanization, which can lead to atrocities. Once we understand our connections, we can move past separatism. On a soul level we are connected, which can and should determine our compassion for each other. No one is above another, no one is above the ethical legal systems we have put in place, no one is beyond compassion.

You can also observe the way you interact with others: Are you looking to gain something from this relationship, or to let others be themselves? When we place judgment, we begin to act as if we are better or separate from those things or people. It is all in the mind, and if it's in your mind and you sense injustice, this is where the fight for the right way is needed. However, you can always find freedom within yourself even if you perceive the injustice of others.

Aristotle and How He Saw Virtue

The idea of virtue ethics is not new, but it helps to know where it came from. The best but most frustrating part of Aristotle's ethics is how his nebulous rules about how to be a better person are really given as a general guideline of what makes you happy. Happy is not the same to the Greek philosopher as it is to the teenager who wants to have sex with everything that moves. For Aristotle, happiness grew from a life well lived, through a feeling of goodness tied to what nourishes a person's soul through virtuous living. Virtuous living was the in-between place, the "Tao" of balance. When you practice mindfulness, you become aware of another observer, what I call "the soul." Within us, in all living things, is an energy that does not just go away. We are not separate, as we are all connected to this common energy. Here is an exercise:

> Silence your mind. Walk outside. Feel your body as you walk. You will notice a tremor around you in the silence. (I feel it within my heart mostly.) Here, your intuition is heightened and you can often have conversations from a place of presence, which allows you to truly hear others. This is the connection we all have.

Tools to Tap into Your Virtuous Self

Historically, religion would provide ethical boundaries for people; however, there are religions that create separation, judgment, and isolation through ideas that push different people away. From an ethical viewpoint, balance and inclusiveness is important. People may not always understand you, but you allow them to be who they are. If you allow them this space, you are more likely to allow yourself space. This is why religion teaches non-judgment. Come from a place of non-judgment and you can see others and who they are.

Eckhart Tolle teaches the idea of living in the present, and not being deceived by the personality, the ego, and reality constructs. Eastern philosophies, spiritual teachers, and philosophers of the past saw the differences between this triangulation of perception. There is the physical and our interpretation of it, which creates our inside dialogue—silence that dialogue and you start to hear, feel and be the essence. This is where you find a spiritual awakening. You may ask, why is this important? Fundamentally, once you can feel your way into the identity of who you are, you become greater than the physical: you are free. Issues arise when we identify with parts of the physical construct, whether in our minds or outside us. Once we release our attachment to these identifications, we free our mind; if we "don't identify with it," we don't become embroiled in the drama, hence why Eckhart Tolle teaches the concept of stopping mind chatter.

Dr. Caroline Leaf indicates that we have a thought every three seconds. A neurologist and researcher, Dr. Leaf works with changing the way we think so we can change our beliefs, and therefore, our lives.[10] The difference between the doctor's work and Eckhart Tolle's is that the doctor is telling you to re-train your mind and brain by utilizing neuroplasticity and mind-over-matter techniques, so emotions and belief systems can be caught at their core; Eckhart Tolle, however, is starting at the beginning, quieting the mind, so you can let your essence come through. I am proposing a bit of both. By quieting the mind and feeling your essence, you can start re-wiring the mind and how it thinks and analyzes situations. Once you come from your essence, you start to see why certain beliefs may have a negative impact on you and those around you.

Your identity does not have to be tied to your mind, thoughts, and beliefs; yet, without structure, you might be inclined to believe you can do anything at a cost to everyone (i.e., like the psychopath who has no empathy). Once you get to your essence, you are now connected with everyone and everything, but it is essential to do away with mind chatter, and start to look at negative belief systems that control your life and the collective.

I once conversed with a peer over lunch at a local restaurant who had just finished her first year of law school (I had not yet applied). She was a highly religious person and was struggling. Law school was challenging her belief systems.

I asked her why she didn't like law school.

She replied, "Law school will change the way you think about everything." She picked up a salt shaker, octagonal with a silver cap, one you find in most diners. "When you see a salt shaker, it's no longer just a salt shaker, it's 'Why is it a salt shaker? What makes it a salt shaker? Is it really a salt shaker?' If you put pepper in it, would it change it from a salt shaker to a pepper shaker? And did it really pull the chair out from Aunt Maisey, causing irreparable damage to her spine, producing a million-dollar tort?"

Okay, the last bit was an illogical leap, but you get the idea behind the Socratic questioning. The Socratic method can be eye opening, freeing, but it can also be soul crushing. After all, what happens when you start to dissect a flower in such a manner? It takes the beauty out of the flower. My friend was having an existential crisis about her religion. Having grown up in a conservative evangelical environment, when your mind is opened in such a manner, EVERYTHING starts to be questioned. This can be unsettling. Your faith in everything is challenged. Yet, being able to look at the world differently excited me—probably because I had grown up in an atheist/agnostic household, with a mother who dabbled in spirituality and a father who was an engineer. The idea of stripping down my belief system in a Nietzsche performative sense gave me chills. Going nihilistic on myself and rebuilding thought processes meant I could rebuild myself. Who wouldn't want to do that?

Atheists will tell you there is nothing other than pure living based on biological structures which are the machinery that makes everything work. Our belief systems are merely constructs so we can handle the world, but fundamentally there is nothing behind them, it's merely functional responsiveness to an environment and we are hard-wired to want stability because we are fearful of things we cannot control. Granted, I would not debate a scientist on this issue without losing, as I too believe this to be the case, and, it has been to our determinant to be controlled by fear. Yet, I have to pause and reflect. The person who challenges my spirituality, my wish to meld spirituality with science, does not bother me because I do not identify with my beliefs as being the only ones someone can hold. I can let the atheist believe in no god and a purely materialistic interpretation of the world. The fact that they call my spirituality a coward's way out does not scare me, does not bother me, because, in the end, you cannot disapprove a benevolent spiritual energy, nor can you prove it. I can only give you my own feeling, perceptions of what I know and see on a daily basis, which have made me trust in something more. So, if you take your belief systems and start to question them, you can open your mind in many different directions. I would propose that the first place to start is to empty the mind through meditation—come from a "zero point." Why? At that point, you are allowing yourself to be reborn, you are not attached, you are not any of your beliefs, you just exist. From there, you can start to unfold.

Chapter 4
Deception as Identity or Agenda

Deception has two forms: (1) what we do to others and (2) what we do to ourselves. It is made up of conclusions we need in order to move our agenda forward. Some people use self-deception to avoid difficult issues; however, if you enter a place where there is no identity and work your way outward (a place where you can layer your identity again and again through experiences, the senses, beliefs, and your ego), you can always tell what your false identity might be. The places where we are triggered want closure. We cannot do that without facing our issues. The people who are best at deceiving others are often the best at deceiving themselves.

In the United States, there are "safe spaces" for marginalized groups (groups that are not in power and that do not have a voice), where they are guarded from criticism. Individuals threatened by this type of space are those in power because it attacks their idea of where they have power. Those in power have, over the years, usurped most areas that *have* voices; hence, it is important for marginalized individuals to have a place where they will not be criticized or bullied so they can be free of deception.

Identity and what we identify with is often dictated by those in power who always have a platform. Historically, those who do not identify with traditional stereotypes of sexual orientation do not have a place to discuss who they are without being berated by criticism. Some people have been marginalized in the United States because of a deep-rooted cultural identification with white males. Hence, in response, these safe spaces tend to be non-inclusive. This is good as it allows a person's personal identity to grow. You will hear things like "people don't change." I disagree with this. Identity is malleable on both a personal and an institutional level. People can change, but we cannot change people. The person must be willing to go deep into their wounds. Eckhart Tolle calls this "the pain body." It is important to investigate your pain body. Jung referred to this as your shadow self. Just like someone has a hero self—the archetype of a hero on their own journey (this can include the anti-hero)—people also have shadow selves: inner places they have identified with a wound they may be unaware of on a conscious level. A wound is often found where someone has wronged us; however, challenge this notion. The only people who "wrong" us depends on our belief of what is "wrong," meaning, if you take away the wrong and forgive the wrongdoing, you no longer identify with it.

Being responsible for our shadow self is crucial in order to break free of archetypes and stereotypes someone imposes on us. Victimhood is an archetype—ask any rescued fairy princess. Historically, women were marginalized into playing the victim. Challenge this. Dig deep and see if this is part of your shadow self. The issue with the shadow self or pain body is that it can be subtle. If you feel victimized, you often project this through judging others: *The "other" is less than me. I am in a superior space.* Nations do this to other nations. Institutions do this to create hierarchies so people will work for them and they can feel justified in their hiring, firing, and marginalization of staff. It is subtle and unequal, and permeates most cultures at some level. After all, if your tribe is less, than my tribe is better than yours.

Ancient western traditions are often entrenched in this idea of manifest destiny which gives rise to superiority and the victimization of others. Yet, when we buy into this system, we take on the victim mentality. Again, this can be subtle; for example, going from judging someone for the color of their skin to judging a woman because she wears no makeup is victimizing. In the end, you are attached to the idea of the victim/abuser. Yet, the reason for judgment is having a sense of powerlessness, either because you fear it might be taken from you as it was in the past, or you have been, and continually are, victimized and you identify with it as part of your pain-body. The pain-body, or attachment to the shadow, is who you have become based on a subconscious attachment to feeling victimized. The bully often plays the victim because their own shadow self identifies with victimhood. In a way, the victim mentality brings power through wound licking; it gives the ego a justification for unfairness in the world.

Every time you judge someone on their looks, you are objectifying them. You are placing them in a victim space. Look deep and see if you were ever the "victim." How did that make you feel? What underlying power created the victim in you? What beliefs did you have that made you feel "less than" since having that experience? Once you start seeing these beliefs for what they are, you can start creating an empowered identity. Once you tap into your empowered energy, you can start changing the inner dialogue and your personal identification. Once you see yourself without labels—hero, victim, or even anti-hero—this is where you can start to find your true identity.

Identification as a Form of Empowerment

"Your turn to serve!"

I looked at the coach and put myself in the corner of the volleyball court. We were playing the best team in our league, a school known for volleyball. We were no longer in the playoff contention, so all pressure was off. I always did an underhand serve. I had a lousy overhead serve. (I really was not good at volleyball, but played it because it was fun.) Any volleyball player worth their salt will tell you an underhand serve is by far a weaker serve as it is easily returned, yet I used it because it was easier for me. However, in that moment, something strange came over me. I can still feel it today. I was in the "zone," laser-focused on making my serve the best underhand serve I could. I did my "bitch-face" frown—ugly but effective for my purpose. I made one serve. The first went in easy and wasn't returned.

Our opponents looked at each other in disbelief: *How could this underhand servy person be getting the best of us, the best dang team on the west coast!*

I did another, and another: five unreturnable serves in a row.

Our opponent's coach shouted in frustration: "Those are easy. Just return them!"

When I heard those words, I suddenly felt bad for the other team. My lack of competitive edge actually made me feel sorry for my opponent. I lost my focus and my next underhand serve went out.

We still won the game, but I had lost my intention and will to serve the "best underhand serves."

Nothing I say here is new to sports psychologists, but my single-focused intention during that game was new to me. I identified with being the best underhand server in the world, and during that game I *was*, much to the chagrin of the opponent's coach and my teammate, Shelly, who glared, "Why didn't you serve like that during the regular season!"

The point of this story is simple: *Where your identification with a passionate intention goes, so does your actual outcome.* Besides, to sports psychologists and new age manifesting spiritualists, "the secret" is not a new idea. However, a person fails when they focus too much on the outcome and not on passion and engagement. If you can convince yourself to *feel* the part, to identify with a particular way of being, you are more likely to manifest your chosen outcome.

In general, I believe a half-hearted, well-intended identification with something you wish to move forward is better than none. If you can work from a place of non-judgment and pure enjoyment, those times are the most remembered, just like the volleyball game from more than 40 years ago that I still remember and feel today. Keeping yourself present, per Eckhart Tolle, allows you to identify with your true self. It requires the ability to be flexible about the outcome. Do not focus too much on what you expect but feel, see, and sense the present moment.

Hatred is Not an Option

Reading philosophy provides a framework for understanding humanity's different interactions in the world. One thing ancient philosophers prided themselves on was rational thinking. For Western philosophers, science, math, even religion, needed to be grounded in an emotional void; after all, how could they save the world if they were wrapped up in emotion? This oppression of emotions meant the dissection of other sentient beings. The oppression of "the other" could be rationalized because "they were better than others." Separateness then becomes an easy foil when someone appears to be emotionally chaotic; after all, children are not usually in control of their emotions so they should be cared for, controlled, taught, and in the most extreme cases, abused because their emotions are out of control.

When writing philosophy, philosophers almost assume a given to that which separates, such as "hatred is a bad thing," yet, they often found ways to justify the marginalization of others, such as women and slaves.[11] However, the way the philosopher thinks, the questioning required in the best Socratic method, gives rise to questioning oppression at all levels.

One aspect that is absent, and maybe to the detriment, is how to deal with emotions. Ancient Greeks saw emotion as detrimental to the rational exploration of the universe. However, modern philosophers, such as Martha Nussbaum, have delved into the emotional aspects of living and how it grows our knowledge.[12] Most philosophers today can see emotion as part of the senses that must be expanded in order to grow our knowledge of the world. After all, human emotions are unique to humans. So, how do we release negative emotions? Hatred, anger, and fear lend themselves to bitterness, self-loathing and resentment, which can leaden our hearts. I use the word "leaden" specifically because if you tune into your heart and feel those emotions which separate us, they are like lead in the body. Say you are angry at your neighbor for parking in front of your house even though you have told them again and again not to. Feel your heart space. Is it light, playful, free? Probably not. Paradoxically, this emotion validates your humanity. We are human because we have emotions. *Be* in these emotions, but when you wallow in them, your outlook on the world becomes one of otherness. If we go back to the example of your neighbor's actions, why does it bother you so much? Is it because they don't respect your feelings, your rights, your freedom? More likely than not, it comes from ideas about your self-autonomy; somehow, it is an infringement on your identity, to our human progress as a whole, but more importantly, these denser emotions keep us stuck in the self-perpetuated identity of otherness and separateness.

Social Justice from Identity

Do you ever notice that when you do not believe in something, what others say about it doesn't bother you? Alternatively, if you believe it to be true (even if negative), you are not triggered by what others say either positively or negatively about you. For example, if you believe you are physically beautiful, if someone calls you ugly you will not care or believe it. Also, if someone calls you ugly and you think it is true, what others say about it will not bother you. Take any trait which society shames or marginalizes. If you believe they are not shameful, you take back your power by transmuting this aspect of yourself into something powerful by no longer being ashamed of it. Shame is a victimhood trait that will not serve you. Once you enter a place of no shame and deconstruct all layers of the personality and ego, and go into your void, you heal shame and work up from there.

Rationally, once you no longer believe in your triggers, you no longer have negative emotions attached to them. A perfect example is Olivia Julianna, who was body shamed by Matt Gaetz, a Republican representative from Florida.[13] When someone feels threatened by another's opinion, slander, marginalization, and manipulation are tools used to keep them quiet. Matt Gaetz said that women protesting the anti-abortion laws looked like "thumbs," implying that no one would want to sleep with them so they would not *need* to have an abortion. (Sexual attractiveness has nothing to do with why someone is raped or has sex and needs an abortion.) Olivia did not allow slander to keep her quiet; she turned it in her favor and raised $1.3 million to provide funds and abortion access through the National Network of Abortion Funds. This is a great example of a woman who was able to leverage slander and marginalization for justice. She told the world she was not a victim. Even though Olivia saw body-shaming as negative, she made it empowering by turning it to everyone's benefit. Empowerment comes from owning triggers and turning them to our advantage. Do not become bitter. Resentment and bitterness make us stuck and overthink. Do not force people to be who you want them to be. Leverage without violence and gain where possible. Make statements that show them how *you* want the world to be.

The Emotional Trigger of Abortion & Logical Reasoning

I am using the topic of abortion to demonstrate how the Socratic dialogue can help us dissect this complicated discussion, as dogma identification and emotional triggers create powerful motivators to control others. Historically, women have died from childbirth at alarming rates. Matt Gaetz's theory makes assumptions that only traditionally attractive people have sex. Also, women and men alike are impacted when bodily autonomy is being taken away. Many people think of abortion as killing a baby. They call themselves pro-life. The ones advocating for a woman's right to choose to see the baby as part of the woman, a tumor of sorts, not yet alive independently. The idea of the religious right is that the baby/innocent needs to be defended, that the baby is alive and independent of its mother. I will explain this position of rational exploration by mentioning comedian Bill Burr's monologue on abortion.[14] To paraphrase, Bill Burr states that a baby is like a cake. Once a cake is in the oven, it is coming out as a cake (a baby). This is a simple and effective use of a rhetorical device to make a seemingly valid comparison; however, let us take this logic to a new level with an imagined Socratic questioning:

"Bill Burr (BB)": "It's in the oven to become a cake."

"Socrates (S)": "Does the cake need the oven to be a cake?"

"BB": "Yes. Because it is baking to become a cake."

"S": "What if the oven is not turned on? Does the cake still become a cake?"

"BB": "No."

"S": "What is the cake while it's in the oven?"

"BB": "It's cake batter, but the intention is for the batter to become a cake if everything is working in the oven."

"S": "But it is cake batter, so really, it's not a cake yet. Isn't it dependent on the oven to become a cake? What if the oven is broken? What if the oven cannot handle the cake because it cannot generate the right amount of heat? What if the batter is the wrong mixture?"

This demonstration provides some context as to why there is a debate. Even if you believe the fetus is going to be a baby in the end, you are presuming it is a baby before it is correctly formed. You cannot assume the baby is a baby—it is batter. This is an emotionally triggering issue but also why the idea of the fetus as separate from a woman's body, and not allowing a woman to make a choice about her own body as an oven, when her body is an integral element, is tenuous logic.

I will present another way people can see that the right to choose is not about the baby at all, but about the woman's body. Pro-life advocates rely on triggering pictures and rhetorical devices to prove a baby is really a baby and the oven is only a secondary in the process of baby making. This is the game they play to assert their agenda; this is why it is imperative to use logical reasoning to see through the agenda. Fundamentally, it is a woman's body. Her right to choose is personal and medical, and should be a decision made between a woman and her doctor—no one else. If you take away personal autonomy of life, liberty, and the pursuit of happiness, you are no longer allowing a personal identity to come to fruition on its own, as it is being influenced by others. It is understandable if people want to prevent the taking of a potential life, but that life cannot outweigh the existing life of the person having the child. It is not logical to weigh a "potential" more heavily than the life of someone who already exists. "Potential" is a possibility, not a certainty. Before birth, the fetus has no identity, no moral code, nor a justifiable existence. It is a clump of cells being brought to life by someone who is already born. Also, if you fundamentally believe in the sanctity of life, then why allow guns? The gun owner may argue that it is their personal right to own a gun, yet when it comes to a woman's body, it is no longer their right? If you are going to be pro-life, you have to be pro-welfare, pro-health care for all, and anti-gun.

What does the abortion argument have to do with identity? Identity is often shaped by our beliefs, and our beliefs are often shaped by dogma, whether religious or scientific, yet I propose *no* dogma should be imposed on someone else. When you take a woman's bodily autonomy away, you are imposing a social dogma that crosses the line: your beliefs being imposed on someone else's life, a life already realized and not a potential.

Identity is often influenced by emotional triggers, which have to do with belief systems; i.e., if you believe fetuses are people, you believe abortion is murder. "Murder must be stopped" is the mantra of Judeo-Christian followers. The emotional pull means you are being influenced by a lack of empathy toward everyone in the situation and you are focused on a potential. When thinking about your identity, look at it closely and decide if you can really make a decision for someone else based on your own emotional trigger. Is it really a good thing to impose your emotional trigger on someone else? Of course, murder is wrong, yet when a woman is making a decision about her own body, it is not our business. The potential of the fetus does not outweigh the privacy and the subjective needs of the woman. Also, women still die giving birth. Fundamentally, a pro-choice advocate could argue, you are sentencing a woman to death by making her take this baby to term, a state-imposed "murder." Logically, there is no justifiable belief system that can weigh a "potential" superior to the reality of something in existence. Even if you are anti-abortion, it is still not your body, it is no one's business. This is the emotionally triggering aspect of moral decisions. Moral decisions are personal.

Where do we draw the line? We can look to moral spectrum ethics; meaning, certain things in our world are morally acceptable while others are not, but on a spectrum, not merely on the pleasure vs. pain spectrum, but on what empowers vs. disempowers and what separates vs. non-separates.

Power as a Moral Definition Within Relationships

I would argue that within our belief system, our sense of doing without, or lack, comes from our desire to gain power: self-empowerment is good; power that separates or confines others is not. Simply put, this is the rule of "do unto others as you would have them do unto you." The desire for power over others—separateness—comes from a lack mentality. Lack is a fear-triggering emotional response that comes from survival instincts. This is where personal identity comes into play. Power is a word that evokes certain fears within people. If we can come to the agreement that all people are created equal, we can also determinate that those "more equal" than others should not exert their power on others. Yet, we cannot have equality within the framework of some people being born more powerful than others; after all, wasn't the U.S. founded after fleeing an out-of-control aristocracy, where people born into power usurped others through their power to tax? Therefore, a morally sound society tries to "equalize" power with certain social programs that raise up and empower the marginalized.

At one point in history, women from PR China were allowed to apply for asylum in the U.S. with the argument that their choice to have a baby was being infringed upon. This served the political agenda of the time, but did not come down to body autonomy in the end. Fallacy identification can be spotted by breaking down assumptions made by different people, entities, and governments. When the Dobbs decision came down, people were shocked; however, it also galvanized people to spot the fallacy of assumptions about women's bodies as being the property of others. We said a woman's right to choose to have children was being infringed upon. This actually came from the evangelical faction of wanting a woman to have her right to give birth as more important than a country's political reasoning. In fact, in China, a woman could have more children if she wanted, but she would be fined. This was considered a fundamental freedom by the U.S. and one which was part of the political persecution; therefore, women could gain a green card through asylum if they wanted more children. The right has changed their tune a lot since then, and so has China. They now allow multiple children because many nations now fear their particular "race" will die out or their economy wouldn't move forward because there wouldn't be enough people to drive the capitalist engine. Think about that deeply: the attack on abortion is actually a "nationalistic" decision of "non-replacement"—this type of dogma latches onto our fears about economic safety but, fundamentally, it is a racist approach. It is the same thing the Nazis advocated: "We will not be replaced." The attack on immigrants, abortion, and a woman's right to choose is a racist viewpoint. People will cloud it with "religion" and "murder," but there is a fundamental elitist attitude about larger populations, where capitalistic barons have their minions at their beck and call for a war against the replacement of its power and dominant race. Interestingly, in the United States, this capitalistic call utilizes migration/immigration for the population decline, until the population becomes too colored, then we have a call for people to stop immigration because we need more "white" people, which can be obtained by stopping women from having a choice. Specifically, evangelical teachings—a dogma—tells us to have children, *lots* of children, which has not seeped into the ideology of the Supreme Court. The Supreme Court has fallen victim to the dogma of conservative idolization. They are so blinded by what a 200-year-old document meant when women had no rights, slavery was the law of the land, and equality only existed for white men. This is problematic. Only when the Supreme Court can release the legal dogma (which is frozen in history), can the Constitution work for everyone.

Capitalism Can Be Equal

Capitalism raises many people out of poverty, but unfettered, the constant fight against monopolies, which do fail, create more oppressive components on a larger scale. Monopolies are capitalism's dictators. A company dogma that insists on conformity and elitism is, in my opinion, a company that will fail as times change. A company that only hires certain people of certain backgrounds fails to be flexible, dynamic, and progressive. Capitalism allows a person in any part of the world to make money by merely getting onto the internet and starting their own business or self-help coaching model. This is where economic freedom exists at its best. That's why, in my opinion, the restrictions on the internet, including taxes on individual developers, should be highly suspect. Creative developers should be able to keep their money without additional taxation. Can we break free? Yes, as long as we utilize the ideas of capitalism on a smaller scale; after all, arguably, once women gained financial freedom, they gained political clout. Being able to work for a living and not be shackled to a man means women can speak up, be heard, and live for themselves.

How Fears Are Contagious, and How to Stop This

The point where technology through Artificial Intelligence (AI) takes over, through its ability to multi-spread and make humanity moot, is not an original thought process as it has to do with "machines" controlling us. (*Space Odyssey* and *The Matrix* are more modern-day versions, but this idea of our material world being an illusion goes back more than 500 years. The difference today is that we are much closer to AI being dominant in our lives.) The idea of technology being our doomsday is based on completely material constructs of how we interact with the world. Rene Descartes tried to dismantle the idea of our thoughts being our controlling perception of the world more than 500 years ago. Of course, the bandwagon of fear of the future—the world's end—is a human construct. We are a sensory perception of our world but, in the end, we become trapped by the perception of being unable to break through this control. However, simply put, if humanity is doomed to experience a technological takeover, we do not have to buy into it. Though we might not be able to walk away from technology, we can walk away with our identity intact because, if our identity is ultimately tied to a spiritual component, we will not be consumed by fear. The ego, tied to our self-preservation, is then no longer the identification marker of our reality. We are freed from the ego, our place of identification; we let go of fear of dying, fear of non-control, through surrender; nothing becomes our master, not our ego nor our perceptions. We walk in the presence of now, with an awareness of everything; we have choices. What others do and say, including technology, no longer has control.

We tend to believe in this overarching narrative of the dystopian society that, for the most part, is being created in the patriarchal interpretation of reality. The patriarch wants to remain in control to ensure things revolve around economic viability. Just like when I talked about the navigation systems of today telling us to do a certain thing, our instincts take over and we say we won't turn into traffic. However, there is more to the survival mode that the materialist does not understand. As we get closer to our technology, if we are in tune with our inner self, the more we will understand. Technology has no control over our internal world. This is where our truth resides and the ego can break free of an egocentric, technologically demanding world.

The real issue becomes how to make AI useful, without losing ourselves in its domination. The death of god and religion has to do with our inability to find the god, the spiritual, within ourselves. That identity, that place of resilience, is more powerful as a feeling of love and empathy than any navigation system. We only surrender our power when we give up making personal choices. If we stop believing everything needs to be dominated, there is no reason to believe technology will reflect our desire for non-dominance, yet, I propose, technology must encompass an ability to empathize and "include." Stephen Hawking, a greatly admired man for good reason, believed in this idea of singularity, but because of our societal modes of interpretation, he brings a few points: AI will reflect a patriarchal conformity of having to control everything. If we switch AI to an empathetic, inclusive thought process, technology could not dominate because it would not need to control anything.

As a feminist and a freethinker, my frustration at the engineer's lack of insight lies in our inability to see beyond the obvious. Technology can only be as arrogant as the person who makes it. *If* the engineering world is dominated by control, exclusivity, elitism, and fear-mongering manipulation, our technology will reflect this—it *has* to. However, if you build a machine that sees the value of humanity as love, kindness, patience, empathy—emotions which do not separate—the machine will not have to dominate because it will reflect those aspects in ourselves. Humans will continue to be, as they have been throughout history, their own worst enemy.

Everywhere, All at Once

Physics knows we live in a multi-verse, so why don't we *feel* into it? Meaning, when we meditate, we can feel the soul's presence and begin to see multi-dimensional possibilities (which has been confirmed by science). So, why go there at all? How does it serve me to believe in this when I cannot see, touch, taste or smell it? Here it becomes problematic because we must be able to see ourselves, not just as bodies, but spirit and emotions. This is where true empowerment lies.

Generally, not understanding the whole means we simply believe technology will take over the world. The categories of oppression mean we do not see our free will as a reflection of our larger selves, our multi-dimensional selves. Men are so entrenched in their hubris, they cannot see greater possibilities. This is why we have experienced a revolution of thought. Millions of people have been oppressed, repressed, and silenced by the arrogance of our need to control. Where we can set ourselves free, people are empowered to find themselves *for* themselves, and not to the detriment of others.

Organized Religion

I grew up in a family of agnostics and atheists; many people I am the closest to are atheists. Atheists are courageous, wonderful, and logical. I say "courageous" because, in the end, they do not believe there is any "help" to do the things they do. They do everything on their own, which means they see themselves as a sort of god with their own belief systems. However, this too can be narrow, as you can pray to the god of science without really understanding what that means. If you were never indoctrinated with a religious upbringing, it is hard to see where you might also have a dogmatic tendency: the belief that your beliefs are better than others. On the other hand, organized religion is also seeped in a way of thinking that can be closed to outsiders. The "our church is better than your church" type of mentality lends itself to exclusivity, elitism, and arrogance, which are all parts of a dogmatic mindset. The dogma mindset means you are so entrenched in your belief system, you come to a narrow place of unacceptance. As aforementioned, ideas that separate, disempower, and are fear-based often lead to arrogance. That said, humbleness is also a form of disempowerment, unless coming from an honest sense of self, or *I am humble because I honestly don't know*. Once you come from a place of humble self-reflection, your mind is opened to other possibilities.

Nietzsche said, "God is dead," but he believed in God. His belief that God is dead came from the need for humanity to rethink possibilities about how to become more self-empowered by leaving behind the cage of repressive thinking. Dogma is another word for repressive thinking. Thinking *I need someone else or some institution to tell me who I am* is steeped in dogma. Religion has done this to many people: believing their religion is better than others. True identity is the enemy of dogma, conformity, and negative constructs. However, you can only get to true identity by not identifying with any particular ideology and by taking the spiritual path. You do not need to believe in a religion or a specific dogma to be a spiritual warrior and find the answers you seek—they are all within. However, none of this is possible without deep self-reflection.

If you have read enough philosophy, a "relative" reality is their thing. Physics and philosophy have come to some point of mergence on this idea of reality being relative to one's experience. However, Descartes proposed this idea several 100 years ago: the dissection of human existence to a point where he proposed, "I think, therefore I am" into a quantifiable matrix where we exist in our own minds—or in Hollywood's terms: in someone else's matrix or computer program. Science is finally stretching itself in this direction. That is the great thing about twiddling thumb thinkers in philosophy. In fact, there was rarely tangible truth to their musings, just logical conclusions based on observations. Simply put, if you sit in a dark room, never see the light of day, have no simulation, no history—just food and water—you will not be tainted by your senses, yet will you still think? Of course, outside simulation, it does not make us not think, it just limits our ability to see different perspectives. That is why people brought up in strict religious groups tend to be intolerant of others' beliefs: they have been taught to think only one way. Yet, it is easy to break through the shackles of dogma with mindfulness practices. Today, mindfulness practices of meditation and observing thought have entered psychological practice, but it all came from a place of philosophical exploration.

Spiritual sources discuss the idea that we are not our thoughts and that they should be observed. However, this is easier said than done because thoughts can invoke a visceral response through triggers from an egocentric existence based mostly on fear and pleasure intertwining, and working to avoid pain by pumping joy into everything. This is what philosophy tries to avoid by looking for a middle point of existence, a balance. From Taoism to Aristotle, the focus has been on the mid-point, the non-reactive point. Your reality may be relative, but your response to it is within your control. Toxic positivity works to deny our feelings and beliefs by not exploring where they came from. Negativity only breeds more negativity and violence, internally or externally. Even though negativity and positivity fall under the same umbrella of human construct, it is not relative if you apply a sliding scale of ethical proportion to empowerment and freedom from structured beliefs. Learning what your beliefs are is easy, being mindful of your beliefs is an intellectual practice; what is not as easy are the feelings attached to the particular beliefs you may have. Also, mindfulness practice is easy—the hard part is bringing that mindfulness into daily living so you can be present and learn to react for the highest good of all involved. Relationships will test your mindfulness, the news will test your mindfulness, and speaking your truth will test other people's beliefs. Yet, if mindfulness is the key, how can you *feel* mindfully? Big beliefs are more problematic; for example, if we accept change as a constant. This becomes easier but the hard part is never being triggered,

not knowing how to respond, or how to speak truth from an empowered practical mindset.

Drug Culture as Dogma

I once made the mistake of getting into a Twitter debate about marijuana not killing anyone (it does not usually lead to an overdose unless it is laced with fentanyl). Not arguing for or against marijuana, I pointed out that, in my neighborhood, otherwise healthy, nonaddicted teenagers were dying because someone was lacing marijuana with fentanyl. My point? When you are attached to a particular thing because it is replacing a hole in your soul, this easily puts you at the mercy of the attitude or belief associated with the addiction. Most drugs, including alcohol, are often used to overcome some sort of pain. The drug can be a prescription, or not. The feeling to overcome is painful, which has a degree of fear attached to it, probably attributable to the fear of dying. Hence, when you caution someone for whom drugs is an obsession, they will get mad at you and attack you as if you were going to take away what is preventing them from dying—not literally, as these drugs are not preventing them from dying, but they are stopping the emotional pain which, in turn, creates a fear of dying from the ego mind. You do not want to get between a substance and the addict.

The person defending marijuana is responding viscerally because they fear someone stopping them from meeting their needs. Yet, where does the "need" come from? Part of the recovery in Alcoholics Anonymous is through spiritual grace. They use spirit, prayer, and meditation as part of their program to recovery. In the end, the ability to process feelings without fear, anger, and repression leads to a form of enlightenment, but first you need to break down your personal addictions by delving deep into your psyche with self-reflection. The same goes for your beliefs. Only through self-reflection can we get to the heart of our beliefs, which can also be addictive. Self-righteous indignation, anger, and resentment can all be addictive. But why? Negativity makes you feel better because *if I can make myself feel I have been wronged, I know I do not have to take responsibility for who I am.* This is not about condoning what or who has wronged you,

DON'T IDENTIFY WITH IT

but about letting it go by freeing your mind from your *addiction* to their "wrongness." The further you can take yourself away from feelings of injustice, the better prepared you will be in addressing "injustices," because resentment, anger, and bitterness disempower you. If you feel disempowered, you may be inclined to want to feel superior by empowering and disempowering others. Ironically, the further away you are from disempowering others, the more empowered you become. Think of it this way: the entrepreneur who seeks to empower their employees will create loyalty from their employees.

Chapter 5

The "T'ude" Limitation

Dogma is more than a set of beliefs—it is the attitude that goes with them. When we make a dogma concrete, we become stuck in it ... we cannot see beyond it. It creates separation because a need arises to be on one road, even if another one would be faster. When I have been persuaded by others' attitudes based on their dogma, I have met the biggest hurdles in my life. My father, an atheist, was anti-attorney basically because he had been sued. Luckily for me, I stretched my beliefs beyond my upbringing to become a believer in spirit *and* an attorney.

A Place of Balance Between Logical and Spiritual Worlds

Taoism is the balance of yin and yang—a small amount of darkness in the light, and a small amount of light in the dark, and the balance in between those worlds. In many ways, balance is living and seeing a middle point in everything. When you start to understand and realize your identity is not tied to how you look, how much you are paid, where you live, and who your friends are, you can move into a place of balance—balance being an observed place. When you silence your mind from all chatter, you begin to look at the world with a different eye. You are no longer a slave to the voices in your head or those around you.

Logic and analytical reasoning play a heavy role in our world. The thinking mind can block us from truly understanding ourselves. Multiple levels of identity are involved: the senses; feelings; and the mind. Some philosophers believe it is only a matter of time till we get to a point where everything can be explained by machines and AI will eventually take over the world. Just as religion can be a dogma, so can science. I do not think AI will take over the world because I fundamentally believe in a soul, the spirit within every living thing. As biological beings, we can tap into universal consciousness and AI. It is what makes us empathize with others. Most of us see death as impending doom; yet, there are people who prefer suicide. Unlike, a human being, a machine could never empathetically "understand" death as a way out because it would have to feel as we do, believe as we do, experience the world as we do. Our biological bodies feel shame, humbleness, and love, which come from a different place of existence; they are not machine-learned. Philosophers have debated about whether a machine could ever fear death. Yes, a machine could fear death if we placed it at a level where the ego became more important to it than the philosophical spirit within it.

If we live in a linear fashion, death comes to us all and hence becomes our release from physical and emotional pain. Yet, we can learn to not be in emotional pain by shutting down our beliefs about it and re-inventing how we think about our external world.

> *I envy those who are dead and gone; they are better off than those who are still alive. But better off than either are those who have never been born, who have never seen the injustice that goes on in this world.* - Ecclesiastes 4:2-3 (GNT)

I am not depressed. I like to get up in the morning and take long walks. I like spending time with my family and my pets, and I like certain aspects of my job. These are all plusses for living; yet, I fundamentally understand why people take their lives. Human suffering is a continuum of survival, pain, survival, pain, a few bits of pleasure, but mostly pain. Most of the pain we experience, once we have gained control of basic survival, is mental. There is a book on the following issue: "Is it better to never have been born?" It quantifies the idea that non-existence is better than existence. [15]

So, what stops us from killing ourselves? Is this a fundamental feeling from our lizard brain that desires life over death? I would argue it is not, for we feel attached to each other and the earth, and a spirit that keeps us needing to be alive. From that viewpoint, we should be so comfortable with our identity that we can find happiness within ourselves, whether that is through serving others, creating, or being part of the larger whole. The "whole" keeps us whole. Even if we are alone, we can feel wholeness if we are willing to tap into it. I am not here to convince you of the existence of god, but to tell you that if you can tap into Universal Consciousness (or Source) you will start to discover truths without understanding where they come from. Clairvoyance is the ability to tap into this realm. Anyone can do it. It is what inspired Leonardo di Vinci to create the famous drawings of the man in a circle with perfect dimensions, or the art on the ceiling of the Sistine Chapel. Tapping into a universal or collective consciousness will expand your mind when you are not trapped in dogma.

Why is there so much evil if there is a god? There are many correct assumptions about others that make life challenging. Yet, when we start to think of a spiritual connection with all things around us, everything makes sense. If we turn our back on power for power's sake, material abundance for material abundance's sake, we begin to see reality as a matrix, a playground—or do we? A playground matrix is only worthwhile if we have something to gain. Or lose. Our soul knows on a deeper level that our existence has meaning. Humanity *seeks* meaning. Not living feels disparate to our spirit. Our consciousness wants to expand. Without life and experience, expansion would be limited. The inner soul cannot be separated from consciousness. Consciousness is not in the mind; it is outside it.

We cannot prove god's existence. Many philosophers have used a deductive reasoning process to do so, starting with a premise that "god is the most perfect being," hence it has to exist because it is perfect and because the imagination cannot create something out of nothing, so there must be a god because we can "imagine it." It is no surprise that a patriarchal thought process was created by a male-dominated religion to support the idea of a "concrete" or "stable and material" god. Think of the Sistine Chapel and the god-like image of a man reaching to touch Adam: there is a gap between god's and Adam's fingers. That is a patriarchal view of the world, not the ethereal aspects of existence—that softer, dreamlike existence you cannot touch, teach, or comprehend without giving away part of your learned behavior. We live within the matrix of our mind. The problem exists in the statement: "God already exists and he is outside of you." If you said, *god exists in my imagination*, this would be a true premise, but it would upset many religious people because the logical conclusion is: *god is imaginary*. Yet, this is the only true conclusion. We can imagine all sorts of things and know they do not exist, such as unicorns. But let us suspend our philosophical thinking within the Socratic teachings of chipping away at logical conclusions based on false premises, and suspend our disbelief for a moment. I will tell you a personal story, one of the first of several intuitive signs I believe came directly from a source energy based on my request.

I was facing a difficult problem and trying to figure out if I had a choice in the matter and whether I was not merely a plaything for god's existence and experience. I wanted a strong sign that this choice was my own. I asked, deeply, for something to appear. In my head, I heard the Peter Gabriel song, "Solsbury Hill":

> Climbing up on Solsbury Hill
> I could see the city light
> Wind was blowing, time stood still
> Eagle flew out of the night…

I was near our team pool waiting for one my children's swimming lessons to finish. Right then, an eagle flew across the middle of it, right past the chair I was sitting in—a beautiful confirmation. The odds of this happening at this time and location are low, as I do not live in a remote area, or in Alaska. Since then, I have been a believer in a spirituality that comes from within. I stopped entertaining atheist beliefs. I live amongst souls—every one of us has that spirit, a deity, the god within us, but we have the choice to find the god or not. Once found, we are never lost again. I am not telling you what to believe, but that you must make a difficult choice—*a choice*—

nonetheless. When you make that choice, do not tell others what or how to believe; you do not have to force your beliefs on others, even if they believed as you did at one time. We have free will.

Since this incident, my belief has been tested and continues to be tested; yet, when I think of things logically—as I am interested in finding a correlation without the rabbit hole of confirmation bias—I always come to the same conclusion: "I know what I saw, and it was beautiful, a confirmation of a question I asked. The song, "Solsbury Hill," is about choices, it is about Gabriel's choice to leave Genesis and start his own career as a solo act." This is also where I left behind the choice of living in a purely academic and/or conformist world and started living from a place of authenticity. Academia likes to create an elite hierarchy based on what is considered worthy according to the current belief system, one that is often non-practical and oppressive to dissenting opinion. In the non-academic world, some people also believe in conspiracies, such as QAnon because these belief systems disempower people (those who believe them disempower themselves and others with their insistence of the dark cabal and believing 7+ million more votes do not count). Modern American culture, to the betterment of many, has knocked down those boundaries through allowing individuals to find freedom of choice at all levels without disempowering others. The very words of how this nation was founded: "life, liberty and the pursuit of happiness," implies a fundamental right to make our own choices. These ideas only become problematic if we believe they only apply to us and no one else.

If we think of this earth plane as full of choices, we become immensely powerful, but it also requires us to think as a community. Our reliance on a patriarchal society to make choices for us comes with only a small amount of responsibility on our end. If we continue to rely on the "father" to do our work for us on a spiritual, political, and social level, we will never be free. In general, there are people who do not relish choice or change or any of the hard work that comes with free will.

Free Will as a Practical Matter

Again, we live in a world of choices. I watch programs about people getting upset because social justice is being brought into STEM. You do not need to believe in social justice, so there is no need to be offended by a social justice question posted to you. Anything that offends you, which does not disempower you or someone else, is usually a problem with *you*; meaning, once you integrate a belief system that stands for an ethically equal society, where everyone has choices, you will not have a dogmatic mindset that says your beliefs are lesser than mine. People's choices are theirs—no one else's—until they infringe on others' rights.

Chapter 6
There Is No Place like Earth

Why are we here? There are myriad ways to answer this question. My take is that we, at the soul level, thought it would be fun and life on earth provides a way for spirit to expand. There is no proof of this, except problematic references to "god's will," "universal design," or scientific evidence that the universe is expanding. We are part of the universe; meaning, we are consciousness expanding. If the universe and everything in it has a purpose to continually change, with the end goal of expanding our awareness, what a better place to do it than one with no reference, where we are placed on a small rock and told, "have at it." Yet, we learn early on that this means we need to work within a system where we are cut off from a spiritual force and have to feel our way around to make sense of our reality: a reality, which, in appearance, wants us to suffer.

Empowerment Is Source's Desire for Us but Not at the Expense of Others

One of the ironies of organized religion, and even "organized philosophy," is that, in a desire to be empowered, there is an idea of "we deserve more than others." Having worked with people of all walks of life, the worst offenders of "power sucking" are found to be men from all cultures and colors. If they feel someone is taking away their power, they dig in and accuse, attack, lie, cheat, vilify, gaslight, and oppress.

Recently, I read a story about a man in a Tesla who drove his family off a cliff.[16] This got me emotionally triggered because, fundamentally, men exist who believe they are worth more than anyone because they were fed this message at a young age. It is a sense of narcissistic entitlement, also championed by some women, either through their own victimhood or sense of entitlement. Think of the white woman in the park who calls the cops on a black man because she is afraid, even though he is doing nothing but bird watching. People behaving badly because they feel they are better than someone else is

DON'T IDENTIFY WITH IT

cross-cultural and comes from not being told "no" at a young age, or alternatively, not seeing the oneness in the universe. If you strip down to the fundamentals of who you are, you can see the oneness of you and others, and hence see the potential for self-actualization in everyone. If you see everyone as having the same rights of respect and intellectual freedom, you no longer impose your beliefs on them. If you see yourself in others, they become as human, as purposeful, as you. As long as you do not believe there is a lack of anything, you will not fall victim to the fear in the lizard brain and take from others.

One of the biggest blocks to seeing others as equal to you is when they don't act, look, or believe the same as you do. This is apparent when I take my morning walks and all the latte moms—blonde, complaining, and well groomed—are hanging together, even though it is a diverse area. I would ask them to organize a block party, but I wouldn't ask them to create the invite list. Having hung around the "latte mom" crowd in small doses, their hidden agenda is always how to get their kids ahead—white privilege is real and women are the gatekeepers. Entitlement makes people lie, cheat, steal, oppress, and disempower to get ahead. Social privilege is justified and created by this dogma of entitlement. We buy into it because we, from our myopic perspective, fear our progeny not getting ahead. We fear our ego not being fed. We fear our space being invaded and being taken from us.

Entitlement comes from fear that something will be taken from me and given to you instead. It is seeped in playground games of who gets to go down the slide first, who gets picked first for the team, and who gets to steal the lunch money from Tommy. Frankly, the dogma of separateness is everywhere, and we need to overcome it to move toward an earth that is inclusive, fair, and diverse.

As there is oppression, disempowerment, entitlement, and elitism or what I call, "separation dogma," people are fighting; hence I believe, to break the cycle, we need to stop our sense of entitlement, which in the end is about separateness. This can be done by first stripping down to our basics, the void within ourselves. Even if you do not find god in the folds of our reality, you can find yourself within, where consciousness lies.

Beware of False Profits

I *love* crystals. One day, I was listening to one of my favorite spiritualists, who sells gems and jewelry. They are beautiful and magnificent, so I bought some. Then I went to Etsy. I was lost—there were so many crystals to choose from. After $500 worth of purchases, I stopped and thought, *what am I doing?* Crystals may have power, they may create more abundance, but in reality...? Spiritual connection comes from within, the rest are belief systems from outside ourselves, just like the Bible can be an addiction. There are plenty of honest and beautiful spiritualists who need to make money to support the distribution of free information they offer. I support them by requesting services when needed. However, I do not believe using "manifesting" and "the divine" to make people buy your product is good ethics, or that what you give out is what you put in: I would not trust someone who sells in this manner. The divine should not be used to instill fear and longing within people, but as a way to empower everyone, not just the seller. The intention of some spiritualists is just like some religions: to make their flock follow them. What is the best way to make someone follow you? Give them a fear-based methodology that uses the divine to hook you. It is the secret to redemption, to manifesting, to being graced, to become superior because you know something someone does not know. It is the FOMO syndrome, where you think someone knows something because they are divinely guided; hence, the spiritualists, the Christian, the whoever, is proselytizing that they know better than you, or worse, they are saying you were divinely guided to their advertisement so you can reap the rewards of their product, at best; at worst, snake oil. Spiritualist peddling is no worse than the weight loss products that flood the market, promising the "ease" of losing weight or getting ripped with their simple secret. In my opinion, the spiritualist who uses fear tactics specifically promises something they cannot deliver without your being willing to buy into a specific dogma. You do not need this. You can achieve it through meditation and the willingness to see your beliefs as potential dogma.

When our institutions and non-institutions, such as spiritualists, come stuck in a dogma of separateness and disempowerment, everyone suffers. When one person becomes embroiled in their own world of "I am the center of the universe and everyone around me is bad," institutions reflect this attitude. This is an oppressive mindset, where my rights are better than yours, you are "lesser" than me and, therefore, do not deserve respect. The dangerous narcissistic attitude permeates from the ground up and vice versa. It was a common occurrence where immigrants to the United States are belittled by immigrants who had come before them—the cycle will continue until someone says, "all are welcome." Right now, we are at a critical stage where people are starting to see the light of welcoming all, allowing people to be who they are as long as they are not hurting others. This can be a short process if we are not married to a dogma of superiority.

As I am always exploring and expanding my desire to get closer to the divine, when the divine is used to sell something, I get irked and saddened. One group I believe to be the biggest "snake oil peddlers" is *The Secret* bunch, the "manifest from nothing" bunch. They remind me of the wholesome image of the show, "The Brady Bunch," where, underneath, they were smoking pot and being unauthentic. Like the snake oil peddlers of old, the only ones getting rich from the manifestations are the ones selling the secret to manifestation. It took a sad turn to my perception of humanity when I learned the very people who believed they are helping others were using the "divine" to make people want to buy their product. They tell you they are giving you a gift: "The divine has guided you to this video (when it is actually an advertisement)—take the quiz, then buy my product to get $10,000 instantly."

The only secret you need to know is that if you get into a good feeling place, with positive emotions, and you express gratitude and say, "I would really like to have $10,000 because I want to go on a trip with my friends," and you start saving, you will likely save faster. Positive thinking and feelings bring you closer to the divine, not paying someone to tell you a "secret" you already know.

Take it from someone who has spent quite a bit of money trying to find god: god is within. Spirit/God/Source bears you no ill, but the responsibility is on you to make your life happy. Source does not care if you have $10,000 or not, but spirit/god/source wants to talk to you, be around you, and wants to see what you discover about yourself. Having a goal in mind, with a daily gratitude marker, will make you feel better in general. You may or may not receive the money, but you will feel a whole lot better in the process. I have manifested quite a bit in my life and I am grateful for it. I set an intention, work toward fulfilling it, and things come to me. Not in a big bang way, but softly through daily work—work I enjoy, which makes all the difference. Be a skeptic by all means, but do not let that become cynicism. Cynicism is the killer of dreams. Where people get the manifestation process wrong, is the insistence that the manifestation must be a certain way; they get attached to the outcome. If you can be in a positive place most of the time, manifesting what you want will come easier, but you need to take some sort of action.

If anyone could tell us how to manifest a winning lottery ticket without giving them $25 or more, we would all be rich. But if you come from an attitude of being rich first (I don't mean spending money you do not have; I mean living your life with the abundance of spirit/god/source and not judging the scenery), you will feel a million dollars better.

Spirit/God/Source is within you, but you must think for yourself. I am not of the spiritualist mindset that the brain is a detriment—I am of the mindset that you must use the brain mindfully.

Dogs are the perfect experiment in mindfulness. Meet "Bunny" from TikTok, who became famous through her owner's development of the talking buttons (https://www.dailymail.co.uk/femail/article-11622989/TikTok-star-pup-asking-anti-depression-medication.html). Some people anthropomorphize dogs, which is the tendency to attribute human qualities to non-humans, such as objects, animals, or phenomena. Anthropomorphizing is a common way humans perceive and interact with the world around them. They want animals to be like them, so they can understand them. We do not need to understand everything from our perspective. Until we let go of the belief that we are the center of everything and believe others have the right to *not* be like us, we will not be happy. Once we start to see the world as a whole—and the world within ourselves—separateness becomes non-optional; it is no longer a dogma we buy into because we see everything as equal, including animals.

How Feelings Drive Dogma

If you are familiar with the witch trials in the United States, you know how the hysteria of witch hunting came from a place of fear, but arguably also from the patriarchies desire to strip women of their property. The dogma was created to establish an outcome by those in power. However, what drove the dogma was the "bandwagon attitude" of *I need to join or I may be left behind or persecuted. I am not a witch, so I need to prevent being labeled one by being on the "right side" of the dogma.* The people who jumped onto the bandwagon of "kill the witch" were being manipulated by an agenda. Power, and the fear of having it taken away, whether it is economic, social, or territorial power, is why people go to war.

Throughout history, power has been, and continues to be, a desire of men to control everything, including women, animals, and nature.

You take because, if you don't, you will be left out. Still, we have a choice to not buy into the dogma once we realize it is a manipulation—

someone's agenda. Most times, if you follow the money, the agenda becomes apparent. In the witch trials, women were getting property; men did not want women to have property because property gives women power. They accused women of witchcraft as an easy way to strip them of that property and power.

Just look around you, the lack mentality is everywhere. People want power because they fear that if they don't have it, someone will come and take their stuff from them. The more people have power, the more we have to share. Do not fall for the dogma; separate yourself from the agenda of the powerful. You are powerful when you realize you can control everything about yourself.

Do Not Identify with Outcomes

Even if you do not believe in god, spirituality, or something within that provides our fundamental purpose in life, there is a point in everyone's life when we question who we are and why we are here. If there is nothing to ground us in this reality, we become lost souls. We can try to fill it with religion, drugs, shopping, entertainment, work, distractions, sex, more drugs, food, or any other means to fill the emptiness within. This will catch up with us. Why do I propose "identification surrender" as a path forward? Because our happiness depends on it. If we do not have expectations, which are created by an identification with outcomes, our feelings will always be hurt. We will continually feel marginalized and in pain from a lack mentality. Shift those mentalities, and we set ourselves free. I will not go into greater detail as Eckhart Tolle's book, *The Power of Now*, on how to be present, is much more comprehensive and focuses on how living in the present releases the need to identify with an outcome.

Identification with the future has often led me to feelings of inadequacy: the *should of, would of, could of*. Because I did not "get this or that" often undermines my feelings of well-being. If you can release the need to identify with who you believe you should be like, and be happy where you are, you can start to move into a more holistic identification of yourself in this world.

Perspectives Are Determined by the Witness in Ourselves; Change That Perspective and Your Witness Is Freed

One of the best kept secrets in our world is that people have their own agendas because their perspectives are unique to their position. The oil man wants more leases on federal land because he believes he needs to drill for more oil to maximize profits. Environmentalists see oil men as greedy, unscrupulous ignorant people who do not care about the earth. These two fundamental dichotomies come from different perspectives of reality. Yet, if they come from those perspectives, neither will come to an agreement about what is best because, logically, what is good for the earth is good for everyone. The perspectives of the "greedy oil men vs. the greater good of the environmentalists" create division. No one sees the middle ground. We identify with our specific agenda so much, we are unwilling to see the humanness of the other.

Energy companies and those who employ them see environmentalists as annoying people who do not care about their jobs or families and want to take away their freedoms. The progressives see themselves as saviors of the planet and the other side as the destructive evasive virus on the face of the earth. If we get away from this identification with what our perspectives are, we are less likely to be triggered by thoughts of "they are going to take my job away" and change it to "let's talk this through and see if a compromise can be found." There are win-win compromises and we do not need to hate anyone to find them.

Negative thought patterns come when we identify with an agenda and see no other values but our own. We cling to this agenda as we try to sort through an uncertain world. If you embrace "not knowing" (uncertainty), and even find it exciting, the need for a specific dogma disappears.

Happiness exists within the balance of two or more conflicting realities. The best way to find it is by being in the present moment and not being emotionally triggered by the world around you. Balance is key to a happy life; yet happiness is elusive because we demand bliss from outside ourselves. Do not look for bliss, look within for your point of balance and bliss will follow. It is not a matter of believing that the world needs to treat you fairly, but rather, being so inwardly grounded, the outside world is merely a playground for a bit of fun. Injustice does not need to be a negative thing, but rather an exciting call to action to change things. Evil is a human construct—so is unfairness, entitlement, equality, and linear time—so throw those ideas out and start with new human constructs that better serve you and those around you. It is astonishing what people can come up with in a collaborative and non-insistent process.

Argument for a Holistic Agenda

Besides Aristotle's proposal for a balanced life of virtue, which argues for a soul-purpose life, there is a need to get in touch with that part of yourself so you are driven toward helping humanity. You may ask, *why should I care*? I suggest that you look deep within yourself and see the likeness of yourself within others, and compassionate action as the force of your soul. You do not need to give up your boundaries to come from this place. Just remember that many people around you suffer. You do not know where they have been and you cannot be responsible for their path, only for your response to them. If your response empowers you, others, and the world around you, you are walking a soulful path.

It takes two for an offense to happen: one must offend; another must be offended. Remove yourself from the drama by choosing to not see the offense. Laugh at yourself, if possible. Boundary-setting provides protection, but real strength comes from not attaching to things people say to you, whether negative or positive. Balance does not need outside affirmations. People's hatred comes from their own wounds. The universe does not wish you ill, nor do you wish the world ill: this is a balanced path.

Unhappiness, anger, hatred, and the lost soul come from a place of pain fed by fearmongering put forth by media or rumors of people trying to make money off that fear. Negative comments on social media, that are not constructive in nature, come from a place of pain or bots programmed to create negative loops because it creates clicks. Take the time to disengage from those platforms and go deep within to find your own answers and do your own research beyond merely "googling something." Do not fall for fearmongering and agenda-driven websites, which are negatively driven by a certain political or social mindset, and news outlets that divide people or distract from factual delivery—they should be questioned.

There is a story of a young woman who lived in a tree for a little over two years to save it from being chopped down by a logging company.[17] The redwood tree was one thousand years old. Long story short, the tree was saved by the young woman, activists, a 200-foot buffer zone around the tree, and $50,000 in funds. The drama began in November 1997 and ended with the agreement to save the tree. However, in November 2000, a vandal, or unknown vandals, took a chain saw to it but failed to cut it down. Why have I brought this up? This incident, for me, is a stark reminder of the political divide in this country: that the young woman was successful in saving the tree, yet someone felt the need to attempt to kill the tree anyway, is just an example of our strange collective inability to find peace with what we see as opposite to our intention.

Progress creates change in people's minds, change creates fear, and fear creates a pain body of more fear. Someone believed the tree represented a political opposition to themselves and their ability to function safely in this world. People damage others all the time when they believe they are being oppressed or disrespected by another group. Luna the tree represented an opposition to the big logging company, and to the locals and loggers who saw their jobs—their livelihood—being interfered with by outsiders. This triggered a reaction within the collective consciousness of the locals toward hating the liberal tree huggers; yet, in the end, the very company who was clearcutting the trees faced bankruptcy due, in part, to their insistence of unsustainable logging practices.

Logically, the locals could only see the immediate disrespect for their ego-borne desire for safety; yet, if they had really thought about the situation, they may have seen the activists were on their side. In some ways, hunters and environmentalists often have a tenuous positive relationship because they see the value of having a sustainable hunting season, which would be impossible if you destroyed the habitat of the fish or deer. ...If only there had been a middle ground possible in all of this, where environmental activists could meet with the loggers to seek a logical compromise.

If you are angry at an injustice, look it in the eye and see if it is triggered by your perspective of entitlement or for the greater good. Once you are involved with a feeling of injustice, you become sidetracked by your personal identification of victimhood. We become burnt out when we identify too much with our feelings and do not look at the practical side of day-to-day choices regarding what we can do now to make our environment better.

Chapter 7
Self-Empowerment Creates Empowerment for Others

My internal dialogue was brave: *I refuse to be weighed. I am not even going to let them do a physical, and I am just getting my thyroid assessed. I am not going to take cholesterol-lowering drugs just to give the prescription drug companies more money to keep me drugged up and placid (or is it flaccid? ...No, that's a Viagra thing...). I don't care if I die from some strange disease this late in life. I'm going to enjoy life and damn the torpedoes. I will tell Dr. What's-It, I've had a long history with doctors, and I don't trust them. They did not catch my thyroid issue before. Doctors don't care about us as people; they only want to make money off our illnesses.*

According to my online health profile for my doctor's office, I *had* to get a physical so the doctor could give me thyroid tests. I was due for my annual check-up, so I had made the appointment, but I was *not* going to get a physical for my thyroid.

The nurse tried her best to get me to do the weigh-in, blood pressure, and temperature check, and she asked me if I wanted to do anything else. I told her I wanted a flu vaccine; she was silent on that. About 30 minutes after my appointment (try to be 30 minutes late in my line of work without massive complaints), the doctor walked in. She was brusque in her behavior toward me when I was adamant about what I wanted. People in authority get annoyed when their authority is challenged, but she agreed to do what I asked—because she *had* to. The interesting thing? She never asked me *why* I had decided not to get a physical for my thyroid. If she had, I could have ranted about the injustice of the medical industry, insurance companies, and the government getting into our business. She didn't give me a chance. Maybe this was her right to do so; yet, wouldn't you want to know why a patient was making this choice? I know this doctor well. I don't trust her. She has gotten things wrong in my chart before; today was no different.

"Looks like you haven't had a thyroid check in a few years," she mumbled—annoyed—

behind her Covid-required mask. This information was incorrect. I had had a test a little over a year ago, which she would have known if she had reviewed my records before my appointment. Unfortunately, my doctor was unwilling to ask a simple question and listen to my response. She did not care enough to know.

Our ego stops us from being curious. It insists on being right, powerful, and oppressive. It is important for those in authority to put their ego aside and ask questions. As a person in authority, do not let your power mindset overpower you. Authentic leadership is not about being self-involved or unable to see beyond your world.

I did not want a physical, though my HMO's electronic AI system wanted me to. All I needed was my doctor to look at my thyroid so my ongoing prescription could be filled. I have had somewhat negative relationships with doctors all my life due to a specific stereotype they have held toward people considered overweight. I am fit and obese according to United States BMI statistics, which are based on "pre-peanut butter and hormone-filled beef" statistics from 1890 and beyond.[18] The BMI statistics, formulated and collected by a mathematician, are now used by life insurance companies to designate a coverage matrix for their clients. In the beginning, it was not a medical industry formulation, but this changed in the 1970s as an easy way for the medical industry to look for other risk factors. The BMI is not reflective of athletic women (at one time, professional and amateur female athletes were rare). Women also did not work out like they do now. Logically, someone who is thin, even if they have an eating disorder, will be considered healthy, whereas a muscular weightlifter or runner may be considered overweight or obese if she has a certain body type.

I do not believe in the medical industry's treatment of overweight patients; hence, I refuse to be weighed. I will not be a body-shaming

DON'T IDENTIFY WITH IT

statistic in the minds of the medical industry. I do not have diabetes, I do not have high blood pressure; I do, however, have a thyroid condition, probably because I starved myself from the age of ten onward. I remember using meal replacement shakes because my dad labeled me as fat. Fat hatred has become a dogma in our society because it makes the diet industry extremely rich. As aforementioned, look for the agenda in a dogma—it is driven by money, not always, but in this case, it has, and it continues to be used to make millions. If we are taught to hate our body, we will try to run from the pain by becoming skinny. For me, it is a trigger that needs to be, and continues to be, healed.

I was able to starve myself to lose weight. Eating disorders do this. I also exercise quite a bit, consistently. Why am I telling you this? Because it is important to not to judge a person by their cover. You do not need to find me physically attractive to respect me; meaning, Aretha Franklin's "R-E-S-P-E-C-T." I take care of myself, but I do not fit into a mold or weight dictated by someone else. Many skinny people die before they are 40, plenty of fat people die, and plenty of regular-sized people do too. I enjoy my life because I am not stuck in the dogma of what society wants me to be. If you are truly enlightened, you will not judge anybody based on how they look.

Having boundaries around yourself means you can say no to authority when it does not serve your life and hinders what you want to do. I did not want to wait 15 minutes, naked, in my doctor's office while I waited for her to say what she wanted to say, which was that I was fat and depressed. She would have known I was eating a mostly plant-based diet if she had read my chart. My attitude about doctors moving forward is: it is my body and when and how I die is up to me, not them.

Food is a form of medicine and so is exercise, so be mindful of what you put in your body, but it's not up to anyone to decide what someone else does with their body. If the doctor gives advice and the patient does not take it, then it is the patient's responsibility to understand the ramifications of their decision.

In the end, I changed my belief system about who I am, from my own perspective of what my body can do, and not what others believe my body should be. Being different in a world that desires conformity is exhausting. Being authentic may make you and others uncomfortable at first, but it will make you happy in the end.

Dogma Blocks Authenticity, Which Takes You Away from Happiness

Dogma or belief systems about how people behave, think, or should be is a form of oppression. Dogma that detracts from your freedom to be authentic is your enemy. It will make you act in certain ways, not from an authentic place, but from fear of not fitting in or not being loved or fulfilled.

Studies have demonstrated that people connected to a spiritual or religious source are happier; yet, if the religious belief is negative (i.e., a god who punishes), the reverse occurs.[19] People become more depressed in such dogmatic environments. An overall negative perception of the world makes a person more negative in general. Yet, it is not simply positivity that provides a buffer to the woes of the world—a less rigid mindset, free from absolute identification with the ego, provides a freedom from oppressive thought patterns. Oppressive thought patterns that identify with a particular belief system will more likely lead to challenges the ego cannot handle, and to a spiritual/philosophical breakdown. Science can do the same and can be just as oppressive.

I distinctly remember: I was about 20 years old and on a trip to England to visit my grandparents. My grandfather had an encyclopedia on his bookshelf that specifically stated that black men had different-sized brains than white people. They cited a study yet, historically, this was not fundamentally true, as was pointed out as early as 1837 by a man named Fredrich Tiedemann.[20] Another researcher named Robert Bennet Bean continued to propose the racist commentary on the differences in brains in blacks and whites in 1907, backed with charts and other material to justify a particular way of thinking. This type of inductive thinking, where someone holds a particular dogma and backs it up with science is dangerous for obvious reasons. The brain's biological differences in black and white people were finally put to rest in 1957, but not until a lot of damage had already been done. During Freud's time, the diagnosis of women as "hysterical" because they were women was also thought to be normal. Labels of women being "overly emotional," because they had a uterus, applied to large swaths of the female population, proposed under science.[21]

I believe science is valid as long as it is based on facts. Bean's research was not based on facts nor was Freud's so-called "science." Both were twisted to fit an agenda that fed an egoic need for superiority and those who supported it.[22] In general, if money flows due to a particular way of thinking, it will get more support by the masses through studies. Think of the tobacco industry, or the lie of election fraud in politics. These industries have used studies to justify making money or gaining power in their respective industries or institutions, whether it is big tobacco or politics.

To close the story about my grandfather—an avid gardener, union member, and extremely fast swimmer—I laughed at this encyclopedia entry and told him it was wrong. He got quite angry. He was comfortable in his identification as a white man and a working-class laborer who could have opened his mind and acknowledged: "I get oppression. I get that black men have been oppressed and they are connected to me," but he lived in his world of racism because, after all, if one wishes to feel better about oneself, one needs to see others as "less than."

The good news is that if you wish to break out of certain ego-identifications, it is easier than ever today. It just takes a bit of discomfort. It is easier to find information that debunks the myths of certain studies out there. You can find the truth. So don't identify with it—don't make a certain way of thinking, being, and a reality yours if it separates, disempowers, or oppresses someone. As with my grandfather, an idea that challenges an ego-based identification will trigger you. If you feel triggered and explore it, it will typically lead you back to an ego identification. This takes work. Some of us do not become enlightened overnight (like me); a few do (like Eckhart Tolle), but this is a journey, not a judgment of *where* we are. If you are called out for doing something, then take ownership, apologize, and move on. If you believe what you did will not create separation at a local or more holistic level, take time to talk to the offended. Do not demonize or dehumanize those who disagree with you because, right now, being offended seems to be an upward trend.

Taking offense is a two-way street. Right now, especially in our political arena, people speak as though they hate each other for their beliefs. Having a strong emotional reaction to something is not bad, as long as it is channeled into a positive solution-oriented direction. Do not be afraid to call someone out on their factual inconsistencies or lies. Propaganda is borne from such ideas and can twist us into thinking we are justified for our outrage when it only separates and disempowers others.

Chapter 8
If We Have Nothing Left to Believe, What Do We Believe?

I have demonstrated the issues around dogma and how it imprisons our minds, so, if we cannot rely on religion, science, or a philosophical guru, where do we find our beliefs? Like all good questions I asked ChatGPT and this is what it said:

> Belief is a personal choice and ultimately depends on your own values and experiences. However, it's generally considered beneficial to have an open-minded and critical approach to belief systems, rather than blindly accepting dogma.
>
> One approach is to adopt a rational and evidence-based approach to belief, where you seek out and evaluate evidence to support your beliefs. This approach can help you avoid being swayed by unproven claims or unfounded beliefs.
>
> Another approach is to embrace a philosophical perspective, such as existentialism or humanism, which can provide a framework for understanding the world and your place in it. These perspectives encourage personal responsibility, self-awareness, and a sense of purpose, without relying on dogma or supernatural beliefs.
>
> Ultimately, the choice of what to believe is yours. It's important to be mindful of your beliefs and to critically evaluate them, rather than blindly accepting dogma. Keep an open mind, be willing to learn and grow, and seek out evidence-based knowledge whenever possible.

Well, that was not helpful: it states the obvious and leaves the rest up to you, hence the fundamental problem with philosophy: the blank slate must be filled, and you get to choose to fill it. You can go with the chatbot solution and let it do your work, but this only scratches the surface. You can be told to believe a fact-based system, but that does not tell you how to treat others, where to create your ethical boundaries, or how to feel good, or anything that makes life worth living. ChatGPT sources information that already exists, but stops at the most critical point: when we ask *why?* Why not accept dogma? Why should we not follow the crowd? The Salem witch trials is enough warning, right? Or, is there something else out there? I think there is: it comes from our ability to see others through our own eyes and understand that we would not want to be treated that way. Many philosophers have come up with ethical guidelines: Aristotle did with his ethical treatises, which ChatGPT tells you about:

> Aristotle's ethical treatises are a collection of works that explore the nature of ethics and moral philosophy. These works include "Nicomachean Ethics," "Eudemian Ethics," and "Magna Moralia."
>
> In these treatises, Aristotle examines the nature of virtue and moral character, and explores how to live a virtuous and fulfilling life. He argues that the ultimate goal of human life is to achieve eudaimonia, or happiness, which he defines as a state of flourishing and well-being.
>
> Aristotle's ethical treatises emphasize the importance of developing virtuous habits and character traits, such as courage, wisdom, and justice, through practice and repetition. He also discusses the role of friendship, pleasure, and contemplation in achieving eudaimonia.
>
> Overall, Aristotle's ethical treatises provide a comprehensive and nuanced exploration of ethical philosophy, and

continue to influence philosophical discussions on ethics and morality to this day.

Fundamentally, Aristotle's ideas concluded that eudaimonia was achieved through a balanced life and developing virtuous character traits. I then asked my newfound technical friend what virtuous habits and character traits were special to humanity. This is what our chatbot said:

> Virtuous habits and character traits are qualities that are considered morally praiseworthy and desirable. According to Aristotle, some of the key virtues that are unique to humanity include:
>
> 1. Rationality: As rational beings, humans have the ability to think critically and make reasoned decisions. Rationality is considered a key virtue because it allows us to act in accordance with reason, rather than giving in to our impulses.
> 2. Courage: Courage is the ability to face danger, pain, or adversity with bravery and fortitude. Aristotle believed that courage was essential for living a virtuous life, as it enables us to stand up for our beliefs and do what is right, even in the face of difficulty.
> 3. Wisdom: Wisdom is the ability to make sound judgments and to apply knowledge to practical situations. It is considered a key virtue because it allows us to make good decisions and to act in accordance with our values.
> 4. Justice: Justice is the virtue of fairness and equality. It involves treating others with respect and giving them what they are due. Aristotle believed that justice was essential for living a virtuous life, as it enables us to act in accordance with our moral principles and to contribute to the well-being of society.

5. Temperance: Temperance is the virtue of self-control and moderation. It involves resisting temptation and living a balanced life. Aristotle believed that temperance was essential for living a virtuous life, as it enables us to avoid excess and to maintain a healthy and balanced lifestyle.

These virtues, according to Aristotle, are essential for living a virtuous and fulfilling life, and they continue to be relevant in modern discussions of ethics and morality.

I then asked my robotic genius: "What did Aristotle say about women?" It replied—expectedly:

Aristotle's views on women were a product of the patriarchal society in which he lived. He believed that women were inferior to men in terms of their intellectual and moral capabilities, and that they were naturally suited for roles that were subordinate to men.

In his work, "Politics," Aristotle argues that women are less rational and less capable of self-control than men, and that they are naturally suited to be ruled by men. He also suggests that women are less courageous than men and that they are naturally predisposed to be more emotional and irrational.

Aristotle also believed that women were suited for domestic and reproductive roles, and that they should be confined to the private sphere of the household. He argued that women should be responsible for managing the household and raising children, while men should be responsible for public life and governance.

While these views may seem outdated and problematic today, it's important to consider them in the context of

DON'T IDENTIFY WITH IT

Aristotle's time and the patriarchal society in which he lived. It's also worth noting that Aristotle's views on women were not universally accepted, and there were other philosophers and thinkers who held more progressive views on gender and women's rights.

The Importance of Taking Historical Context and Dogma into Account

Ironic, right? The man espousing virtuous living decided the moral compass of his day dictated his thoughts about 50% of the population. Did Aristotle bother asking *why* he should believe women to be inferior? He passed judgment and stated his reasoning as if it were fact. Questioning why you have a particular belief system is essential for development, creativity, and growth. Why is it believed that Chicago has a high crime rate? Is this based on fact or repetition in the media ("Chicago is the murder capital of the world"? It is not.)? We are captured by fear, and fear creates a need for safety, and safety requires judgments and conclusions shaped by beliefs that keep us safe. We are not safe if we stay afraid. Fear is only a tool governments and the media use to keep us under control. Breaking free from the dogma created by fear—fear which separates and blinds us to truth—is the only way out of our problems.

What ethical framework should you follow? I suggest you look within and see where your thought processes lead you. Says ChatGPT:

> There are several ethical frameworks that make sense in today's society, depending on one's values and beliefs. Some of the most widely recognized ethical frameworks include:
>
> 1. Utilitarianism: Utilitarianism is an ethical framework that emphasizes the greatest good for the greatest number of people. It seeks to maximize happiness and minimize suffering for society as a whole, and it is often used in public

policy and decision-making.
2. Deontological ethics: Deontological ethics is an ethical framework that focuses on duty and obligation. It asserts that certain actions are inherently right or wrong, regardless of their consequences. This framework is often used in professional codes of ethics, such as those used in medicine or law.
3. Virtue ethics: Virtue ethics is an ethical framework that emphasizes the development of virtuous character traits, such as honesty, courage, and compassion. It focuses on the individual's character rather than specific actions, and it is often used in personal decision-making and self-improvement.
4. Care ethics: Care ethics is an ethical framework that emphasizes the importance of caring for others, especially those who are vulnerable or marginalized. It focuses on relationships and empathy, and it is often used in feminist ethics and bioethics.
5. Human rights: Human rights are a set of principles that assert that all people are entitled to certain basic rights and freedoms, such as the right to life, liberty, and equality. This framework is often used in international law and political philosophy.

Ultimately, the most appropriate ethical framework will depend on one's values, beliefs, and context. It's important to consider multiple ethical frameworks and to engage in critical reflection and dialogue when making ethical decisions.

ChatGPT provides a plethora of information about different schools of ethics. Suffice it to say, beliefs that separate, marginalize, oppress, and suppress lead to injustices. The human traits of empathy, kindness, inclusiveness, elevating others, altruism, rationality, and love provide us with ethical frameworks for how we treat others. Anything that separates and oppresses, such as hatred, nationalism, exclusiveness, bias, greed, violence, and dehumanization comes mostly from a fear-based dogma, much like patriarchal structures of old. Breaking down any dogma that has dominated a society and dictated societal norms takes quite a bit of work. Yet, individually, if we can start to see where we can break free from our own mindset about certain aspects of human likes, dislikes, and attitudes, we can sometimes find a common core in our beliefs, which is conducive to learning, opening our minds, and critical thought processes. I propose focusing on those things that bring us together (and do not separate us) as a healthy consideration for better living.

Unfortunately, a wide swath of philosophical teachings, from ancient to more modern times, including Immanuel Kant's, proposed some sexist, racist views. You need to cherry-pick amongst most ancient teachings to find those based on equality. The funny thing about ChatGPT is that if you ask general questions about philosophy, you will get some basic answers that whitewash some philosophers' ideas. For example, ChatGPT answered the following question about which philosophical teachings believed in equality for all, regardless of race:

> The concept of equality for all, regardless of race, is a relatively modern concept that emerged in response to the historical and ongoing injustices suffered by marginalized groups, including people of color. However, there are several philosophical teachings and movements that have promoted the idea of universal equality and human rights that extend beyond racial boundaries.
>
> One such philosophical movement is the Enlightenment, which emerged in Europe during the 17th and 18th centuries. The Enlightenment was characterized by a focus

on reason, individualism, and the rejection of traditional authority. Many Enlightenment thinkers, such as John Locke and Immanuel Kant, believed that all humans possess inherent rights and freedoms that should be protected by society and the state. This idea of universal human rights and dignity was a major inspiration for the modern concept of equality, and played a significant role in the development of liberal democracy and the abolition of slavery.

Yet when you ask "what did Immanuel Kant think of black people," ChatGPT provides the following response:

"Immanuel Kant, a German philosopher who lived from 1724 to 1804, expressed some controversial and problematic views on race, including black people, in his writings.

Kant's views on race are mainly found in his anthropological writings, such as his 1775 essay "On the Different Races of Human Beings." In this essay, Kant divides human beings into four races based on their physical characteristics, and asserts that the white race is superior to the others in terms of moral and intellectual capacity.

Kant also makes derogatory comments about black people, describing them as "uneducable," "lazy," and "stupid." He argues that black people are "far below" the other races in terms of their intellectual and moral capacities, and that they are incapable of achieving the same level of civilization and culture as the white race.

At this moment, I ask the reader to pause. Let's take the passage above and change it up: "Kant also made derogatory comments about white people, describing them as 'uneducable,' 'lazy,' and 'stupid.' He argues that white people are 'far below' the other races in terms of their intellectual and moral capacities, and that they are incapable of achieving the same level of civilization and culture as the black race." Interesting.

You can blow your mind by challenging assumptions through mixing up the language used about someone who is being marginalized. You use your race, or another attribute, and place those unchangeable characteristics in the "judgment box." Let yourself really feel what it is like to sense the pain of those words when applied to you. Maybe "white" isn't a trigger for you; in that case, try something else and see how it feels.

I do not ask you to do this to attack your self-esteem, but to help you sense how being labeled, judged, and dismissed feels to others. Another way to do this is to take something that makes you feel inferior or not worthy. You can try this with any physical attribute you are sensitive about and see how it makes you feel—it will hurt you emotionally if you do it right. The reason to practice this experiment with your trigger points is not to make you a victim, but to empower your sense of empathy. Empathy is a superpower.

The takeaway of my rant against Kant is that he, who some would call the father of modern philosophy, was racist. ChatGPT is only as good as the sources it accesses, and if there is a lack of diverse sources, it will also demonstrate bias. The questions to ask demonstrate to the reader a systemic bias in what we are being taught. If I had not known about Immanuel Kant's views on the black race, I would not have been able to ask about his beliefs about other races. You have to specifically ask ChatGPT about historical factual data, which only comes about because of previous education, otherwise you will not get the full picture. We cannot whitewash history. Our western beliefs, our fundamental educational systems, create a lack of understanding when we purport to see the whole for only part of history. We can label Kant as "enlightened for his time," but he was not an advocate of "equality for all" because he did not, at a basic level, believe everyone should be accorded "equal status as humans." This creates inequity and systemic historical bias about who has been heard and who continues to be heard. If you can dehumanize others, you do not need to accord them respect, or even life.

So how can we balance our historical biases with a forward-thinking notion of enlightenment, without a systemic bias toward those who, in hindsight, were not progressive? We need to ask questions about the labeled and ostracized—about their ideas. How can we incorporate their ideas into today's philosophy? The problem with relying on the dominant philosophical teachings from history is that we lose our ability to think beyond systemic bias. I go back to the Chairman of the Joint Chiefs of Staff, Mike Mullen, who said "ducks hire ducks," which presents the idea that white men will elevate white men in the military, which applies to all aspects of society, for whoever is doing the hiring, the elevating, and idea making. All these areas are going to be controlled by where we have been, and not where we are going, unless we look history in the face and see reality for what it is.

Asian philosophical traditions, specifically Taoism and Confucianism, provide some fundamental tenets that avoid judgments about race, gender, and social hierarchy by leaning toward the basics of human decency. ChatGPT states:

> Confucius' teachings primarily focused on the values and behaviors that lead to social harmony and personal excellence, such as filial piety, respect for authority, and the pursuit of knowledge and self-improvement.
>
> In Confucian thought, people are judged based on their character and actions, rather than their physical attributes or ethnic background. Confucius believed that all people had the potential to be virtuous and contribute to society, regardless of their social status or background.

...and ChatGPT, on Taoism:

> Taoism also emphasizes the importance of simplicity and humility, which are seen as virtues that lead to greater harmony with the Tao. These values suggest that we should not judge others based on their social status or wealth, and that we should treat everyone with the same level of respect and kindness.
>
> Overall, while Taoism does not have a specific doctrine of equality, its teachings emphasize the interconnection and equality of all beings, and encourage a compassionate and humble approach to life that values harmony and balance over individual achievement or domination.

Basically, these ancient tenets create a form of equality by looking into the practices of compassion, harmony, and balance. Maybe if we pause and reflect on where we have been, especially in western philosophical and dominant thought, we can see the value in opening up the conversations to others to provide a forum for seeing the potential of all from their own perspective.

Chapter 9
The Matrix and the Blue Pill

One advantage of philosophy is that it allows for musings; yet, this is also a disadvantage—after all, the famous armchair philosophers of yesteryear were primarily interested in laying a foundation for dismantling how we are *assumed to think*. The disadvantage is based on factual discussions made by "smarter/scientific" people—that has become apparent in the academic world. For example, take the most recent discussions about different frameworks of our world merely being a mind-simulation. Brilliant minds say that there is a 50/50 chance we have all swallowed the blue pill.[23] Meta-physicists have been saying this for a long time, but more importantly, over 300 years ago, Descartes (1596–1650), a French philosopher, came to a similar conclusion that questions our material existence based on the sensory world—even the internal world can fool a person.

Descartes' conclusions came from a place of inquiry. He was able to deconstruct reality with his questioning. This is the beauty of philosophy: using logic, you can often reduce ideas into theories to be further explored; yet, at this time in history, there were no physicists saying that we live in a simulated world. In the end, Descartes muttered those famous words: "I think, therefore I am," the idea being that, when we think, we deconstruct our existence through inquiry and therefore know we exist. Like Neo, , *The Matrix*'s main character, Descartes saw the world around him as malleable from a sensory perspective—not concrete, not tangible—because sensory perspectives are misleading. Like *The Matrix*, Descartes' world is not solid. In the end, Neo wanted truth above all else. I, too, believe in this. The truth often makes people uncomfortable. Some people will tell you they have the "truth," however, be careful of false prophets. They will tell you things that seem "off" because, logically, they make no sense: "JFK is being resurrected," "the election was stolen," "Trump is your savior," but conspiracies are not truth-finding; someone is making money off them.

Conspiracies are cognitive biases made by making connections between tenuous and unrelated facts. I will give you an example...

...There is a big conspiracy about a "new world order," where a group of rich families are coming together to take away your money and power. There was a speech by George W. H. Bush back in the '90s, which talked about the new world order; so did Ronald Reagan in the '80s. These ideas promoted world democracy and peace on a global level through the U.S. supporting these ideals. Over time, the idea of a new world order became twisted into a global cabal of influencers whose nefarious dealings include reducing the population through mass killings, among other things.

Fundamentally, the idea of a group of global elitists possesses a degree of factual basis. Worldwide, there are wealthy and powerful people and families who possess a disproportionate amount of all wealth (Oxfam's 2020 annual report said that the world's 2153 billionaires hold more wealth than the bottom 4.6 billion people). Do these people have more power and influence? Yes. Do they find ways to keep their power and money? Yes. But they are not "lizard people" controlling the media from behind the scenes though they might be stuck in their lizard brains. The rich and powerful are not out to kill everyone off. Logically, why would they do that? They need people to work for them.

The perception of an evil cabal of powerful people has a kernel of truth to it, but it is based on fear. The Nazis gained power by using fear. They pushed their agenda of mass genocide by using the "us vs. them" mantra. Watch the fear in yourself and others; be aware of your buttons being pushed and your triggers.

The problem in our country is that we tend to believe the conspiracies because no one tells us otherwise. You create your own echo chamber by doing your own research and finding like-minded people. Some would say it is our educational system failing to raise critical thinkers. It is also because money creates gatekeeping at higher learning institutions. Right now, a year of tuition at most colleges is the equivalent of buying a luxury sedan every year. It is up to community colleges to educate the masses after high school, yet they are becoming more and more expensive. We are coming from a place of pain and disillusionment in the United States, as we are told that everyone is created equal, that everyone has the right to life, liberty, and property. People of color know the "equal opportunity clause" has been a lie for a long time. White people are waking up to it, first by blaming people of color and those different from them, like immigrants. When we fear we are losing, we tend to close ranks with like-minded people; we identify with them, and their dogma becomes ours: *What I have is mine. I need to go first. I need to be first. I am dispassionately unaccepted, so I need to be accepted through my dogma of lack, and I blame others at the expense of inner peace.* In the end, people find a way to belong, which is to find like-minded people who blame others for their misfortune.

Repeating a lie multiple times does not make it true; hence why, from a practical perspective, doubt helps (this was Descartes' paradigm), but in the end, look to agendas that separate through the demonization of others, through money-making schemes, fear, and our truth as a family. Being interconnected relies on seeing through and using critical thinking skills, but not at the expense of others. This sets you free. What is difficult with truth finding is that the amount of information available, and the manipulation of facts, can give an overwhelming sense of despair. This is why it is imperative to see who is presenting these facts, where they are coming from, what their agenda is, and asking if it is for the common good, if it will help someone along their path, or if it is merely to make money for themselves. I think funds in the hands of the few create inequalities, injustices, and violence, but it is systemic—and people are catching on—not about a new world order, but about how our country is geared to making money and making it off the backs of others. In fact, many capitalists are now saying the birth rate is down and we need to make sure we have enough workers in the future. I heard one young lady with a childfree intention declare: "I'm not concerned about breeding kids for our future economy. Why would I do that? So my progeny can work in jobs they don't like, for others to be wealthy and drive Maseratis?" The thought processes of many of these young women come from a place of: *If the world is full of violence and poverty, why should I bless the world with my children?* That is something for corporate America to take into account. Young women abstaining from having children are making corporate America uncomfortable. Being uncomfortable is good for people; it makes us think. Being disruptive of social norms is not violent when it comes from a place of love. These women are speaking out against hatred and violence by stating their truth and they get judged for it.

The famous paper by David Benatar (1997) titled, "Why It Is Better Never to Come into Existence," supports the idea that there is more pain in existing than not existing. It hence would support the idea of women not having children. In fact, he proposes it is selfish to have children because, fundamentally, you are really having them for yourself, though existing is painful. It's ironic that if you think of existence as painful, your desire to have no children is actually a selfless act.

We Live in a Matrix Built by the Powerful and Rich for Their Benefit

Most physicists would say we are all energy and we create our own reality. Fundamentally, the manifesting bunch (think: *The Secret*) would have you believe you can just shift your reality within the matrix and manifest anything you want. Those who proport to have a secret are making money off their secret because they are telling you *they have a secret*. They say it is all about your vibration, your vibration creates your reality, etc. This is true, but only to a point. Your perspective creates your reality, not your vibration; and your feelings are what create your perspective. Last time I looked, I had to walk across the road to get to the other side. There was a road, there was another side, and those were physical. So, practically speaking, the creation of "my own reality" is not very helpful. There is a physical reality around us. The simulation idea, although fun to think about, is not helpful for navigating day-to-day living. If I eat a donut, my cells are still going to go into sugar shock and scream their resistance to my being unkind to them—hence why I cannot *feel* myself into eating a donut being good for me. Feeling good helps, and mantras help keep you on track to creating your dreams, but they are not the only answer. Action creates momentum, which creates your reality. Thoughts and feelings are part of our world, but only if we choose to make them so. You cannot *will* away bad things that have happened, but you *can* shift your suffering from a victim mentality to a power mentality and feel better. Which is more helpful? Seeing the world as against you, or as supporting you?

What philosophical discourse provides is a practical application of our response to our reality. One thing we have at the level of daily living is free choice to take daily actions. Yet, a new trend to point out toxic positivity, or the "lucky girl syndrome," allows us to question the idea of "faking it until you make it." Positive thinking and attitudes will get you places as long as you really feel it, but only if you also possess attainable ambitions around your manifestations. Have fun with it, but it is not your fault if it does not turn out the way you think it should. Let go of identifying with an outcome.

Freedom of Choice is the Ultimate Freedom

Some would argue that there is no free will in the choices we make, that everything has a pre-determined outcome due to what came before it (aka, the butterfly effect); yet, is that helpful? No, because you would do nothing with your life or with the reality around you. Depending on your beliefs, you would constantly think: "If I do this...will I hurt someone?" You cannot carry that amount of responsibility for the world around you—nothing would work—yet, we must take responsibility or nothing *would ever* work. For instance, Steve Jobs was an innovator, but he was not a humanistic/ethical genius until it served him. He offered the world great technology off the sweat of those who worked for him. When he was getting older, he concluded that "a watch, no matter how much it costs, still tells the same time" or "a car, no matter how much it costs, still gets you to where you want to go." (Most people who live at the poverty line have that figured out.) These are not epiphanies of a caring person. Jobs was more interested in screwing his friends over, or suppressing technology, than making the world a better place. He did create changes in his company to process computer junk for environmental reasons, but he had already created the toxic stuff in the first place. "Tech bros" create the crumbling building and then ask someone else to stop it from falling. They may be incredible engineers and cutthroat leaders, but the rest of humanity is there to buy their product, whether it is useful or not. When decent humans with massive resources see a problem facing others' basic needs, they put aside their egos and look for solutions. They stop and talk to people in need, see others' humanity, and seek to elevate—not demean, disempower, or suppress.

The red pill of truth? It is where you can start seeing the world from a different perspective. I would surmise that most people do not believe in a simulated environment, and maybe they do not believe in a different perspective as being a plausible alternative reality. After all, perspective is narrow in scope. It is not that there is no road to cross to get to the other side, it is just that the road may seem a harsher color, a rockier surface, or even not worthy of crossing. Compare this to someone who might see the road as something not worth thinking about in great detail. "Right" answers do not exist in the realm of perspective, except you can use a sliding scale of ethical deduction to determine what is for your, and the greater, good. You are less likely to judge others if you come from an open perspective devoid of dogma.

Truth can be found by pulling the plug on our beliefs, perspectives, and biases. Returning to the core of who we are, and creating our perception of our reality, comes from seeing things from a different perspective. I am not big on reality being as malleable as a physicist or Neo might think, but I am about changing the way we interact so we can have decent discussions with each other. Our country is divided because we get entrenched in our beliefs and scream at each other instead of trying to understand each other. Though this does take time, if we are interested in having a decent discussion with others and want to make our environment better for all, we can come to a place of mutual respect when we release our biases.

Though sense perception confuses us at best and deludes us at worst, we are ultimately in control of how we perceive things. In the legal field, eyewitness testimony is most precarious because someone else has a different view. Once you open your mind and stop being closed off to other perspectives, you are no longer confined to your own reality, but start to see the realities of other people.

How to Spot Ego-Play in Others and Yourself

It is easier to spot the ego driving your reaction in yourself than it is in others. The ego is not bad, but it can derail you into delusions and cross-purposes. On a simple note, the egoic self refuses to ask for directions because it does not want to look like it doesn't know where it is going. On a grander scale, it insists that you can drill oil in an area where deep sea animals will die from the environmental change.

When you are hurt by something said in a social media comment, that is your ego reacting. One of the biggest challenges to daily living as a human today is the unkind things people say. If you do not believe the unkind words are true, they will not impact you. If you fundamentally believe they are true, but you embrace this part of yourself as beautiful, your ego will not care. Your ego responds to things that trigger because of a past trauma or hurt. I would not ignore these feelings, nor would I wallow in them. Be okay if the trigger comes up every so often. That is what living is about. We are perfect as we are; we are not here on earth to experience perfection.

Though we may need to judge someone when they are hurting others, discernment about what is "good vs. bad" is very important; however, being judge, jury, and executioner is ego-play. Our ego is playing a game of chess where it makes all the moves and decides the outcome because that bolsters its importance to us. However, we have absolute control over our ego—it is not a disembodied play piece.

The Inability to Process Disappointment Is a Form of Disempowerment

DON'T IDENTIFY WITH IT

You might ask: "How is my inability to process disappointment a form of disempowerment?" If you think of someone who is always told they are great and the world is their oyster, success at all costs becomes their belief system. Everything that motivates them comes from a place of how to get ahead because they need to be the best, and if they are not, they may have a mental breakdown. This happens to many successful people. To avoid the pain of disappointment, they work to achieve hyper-success by any means possible: cheating, "criming," or some other means. However, this can be subtle. I will take you through a certain scenario that recently happened at a prestigious swim competition...

Swim times and swim meets, like many sports in the U.S., have become hypercompetitive. A particular private all-girls high school, now very well known for their sports, decided to forego one of the relay events. This meet is what determines high school placement in the state swim competitions and has the means to get students into the college of their choice because the stakes, the times, and the prestige, are high. The swim coach decided not to do a certain medley (IM) relay because the coach believed the team did not have a strong backstroker. The event requires that each person on the relay team do a particular stroke: backstroke; breaststroke; butterfly; or freestyle. The girls from the team could not make a good enough time. They would have made the finals but would not have been placed in the top three. The swim coach decided to have the girls race in the 200-freestyle relay, not the IM relay. This move did not teach these privileged young women (the school tuition is the same or more expensive than some private colleges) that people sometimes lose. Learning to deal with disappointment is an important life lesson. The coach, maybe well-meaning on some level, actually disempowered these young women by not allowing them to experience a loss, learn to overcome it, and have good sportsmanship. Ironically (or through karma), their team was disqualified because a swimmer left the blocks too soon.

That example is just one simple way adults sometimes get in the way of children learning how to deal with disappointment and how to move on. It is the same as giving every child a participation trophy or medal. The fact that we live in a meritocracy means we sometimes do not get what we want. It has been sung about and said for eons, that in a land of opportunity, the fact that we have opportunities, and don't try, creates a society of people who only identify with results and not actual experiences and processes in life. Focusing on results or identifying with the outcome means we cannot enjoy the moment. We disempower ourselves by not living fully through experiencing what life throws at us, whether it is disappointments or wins.

Practically speaking, if it helps you to think that we live in a matrix, then make it a positive one: here, you strip down your beliefs by identifying with those that separate you from others and truly come from a place of mindful interconnection. You would never yell at anyone, there would be no need for boundaries, there would no longer be anger, hatred, or judgment. I would use the word *love* here, but it tends to be overused. I prefer the words *compassion* and *empathy*. You might not be able to walk in everyone's shoes, but you can be curious about why someone might believe in what they do.

One of my biggest hurdles to accepting of others for violence, for war—for all of it—is judging. This is tricky because, on one hand, we have to make discernments when looking at the world and speak up when there is injustice. Generally, most people would like to live in a world of peace, no drama, and understanding. Yet, let us be frank: when there is no justice, there is no peace. Each of us is interconnected, and if another human is being harmed, we are all being harmed. This is hard to fathom, but physicists will tell you that the harder you look at the material world, the less material it becomes, and the more energy and space there is within ourselves and others. This energy is interconnected and never dies. Think of that: *energy never dies*. Our ability to connect to the energy around us has been practiced for

DON'T IDENTIFY WITH IT

centuries by Qigong masters (also mentioned as "the force" in *Star Wars* on a somewhat superficial level). For my purposes, I perceive this interconnection as a "source energy." It does not matter what you call it, but it is around us in everything—from the ecstasy of bliss to the pain of a broken limb, it is energy being emoted, exposed, and felt by us.

When we disassociate from the pain of another, we are disassociating from this source energy. Yet, how do we survive in a world where there is seemingly pain everywhere? Fundamentally, you cannot help everyone, you cannot walk in everyone's shoes, but you can support and connect by listening, questioning, and engaging with the world around you. This means you connect to source energy in everyday living without becoming overwhelmed by the world's problems. Remember: "to teach someone to fish is much better than giving them the fish." Still, by sharing your knowledge, learning, and abilities with others at a fundamental 1:1 level, you are impacting this person more than you can imagine. We know this to be true. When you smile at someone and they smile back, they will smile at someone else, and so on, and so on.

On the reverse side, is cruelty. There are people in this world who are bullies, who will take your lunch money and will be cruel for the sake of being cruel. We stand up to them in an ideal world. This is why we are in the world, to make it better for others, but also ourselves. Don't be the bully to yourself either.

Bullies suck.

Trump is a bully.

Therefore, Trump sucks.

See how I did that? You can potentially fight me on whether the premise of "Trump being a bully" is accurate, but I will say he was found liable for sexual assault in a court of law. Sexual assault is a bully's game, as you aren't interested in anyone's empowerment and you take from others without consent, which is pretty much the definition of a bully. Let's see what ChatGPT has to say:

> It's important to note that the perception of Trump as a bully or not is subjective and varies among individuals. Public opinion on this matter is divided, and different people may have different interpretations of his behavior and rhetoric.

According to ChatGPT, there is a subjective interpretation of Trump's actions—and it is not going to have an opinion. Interesting point; yet, reasoning defies this idea if there is evidence present that would suggest otherwise. Why anyone would not conclude that someone is a bully when evidence presented suggests otherwise belies the practical application of the AI tool. I know for a fact that AI gets some of the nuanced practicalities wrong; therefore, I don't believe the ChatGPT to be right in this instance.

Now you could say: "But you are being a hypocrite. You are closing your mind off from the possibility that you are wrong?" I would answer: "I am using my discernment to make a determination about Trump's actions of name-calling, making fun of people, and sexual assault, which would demonstrate someone who does not care for others and just takes what he wants." Interestingly, after I asked more probing questions, the ChatGPT admitted that the news source and information it had gathered was on or before September 2021, so it did not have knowledge of the sexual assault issue.

The AI system does not want to slip into the political spectrum of opinion in general, which is probably a good idea. However, this makes it essential for us to know enough to question the perspectives given in ChatGPT. The danger of not drawing boundaries could result in clouded opinions and different perspectives where we don't know the difference between good and bad.

Chapter 10
Opinions—Everyone Has One

Opinions are everywhere, so make yours a good one. If you are going to identify with someone as a mentor, or see an idea as worthwhile, make sure it is good. From the day we are born, we gravitate toward an opinion. We do not like the pain of hunger or thirst, so we cry and scream until this is resolved. Pain makes us reject certain things. Pleasure makes us want the binky, the warm blanket, a hug. Arguably, these first senses come from our basic need to survive. Hunger and thirst need to be quenched or we wouldn't make it through the year.

Do pleasure and pain drive our opinions about everything? Potentially, this is true. For example, if I remember great pleasure in my mother providing me with sustenance over time, I will have an opinion that all mothers are wonderful because they fulfill this need. This opinion is based on a "feeling" received from comfort: pleasure. Yet, not all mothers are going to be wonderful. In the end, a good feeling does not necessarily drive a "good opinion." I may feel good about "being superior to others" because, at a young age, I was wounded from not being accepted. To stop myself from feeling the pain of rejection, I work hard to be successful, and this gives me a feeling of superiority. Hence, my opinion of being superior comes from a place of pain. Believing you are superior to anyone breeds separation from the whole.

I once talked to a young man who was educated at Eaton and Stanford. Though highly educated, he wasn't very enlightened and needed to feel he belonged to a special group. When Facebook was first launched, and before it was a national platform, it was only for Ivy League or equivalent schools—Stanford being one of them. The young man liked Facebook because he felt he belonged to an exclusive club; he said this was what made it a great platform. Exclusivity makes people feel good because they identify with a tribe. This person was also an Indian national and had come from a caste culture.[24] These ingrained inequalities from his culture[25] may have been reflective in his desire for exclusivity which, although probably unintentional, basically "excludes others for the betterment of others." I thought it was strange that he openly liked the idea of exclusion, as if being an elitist was a good thing. This undermines striving toward equality and freedom for all in the United States. Of course, this is my opinion about what drove him to desire exclusivity, especially his being an immigrant and person of color, which I am not. However, with the colonialism of India by the British Empire, you would have thought it would have bred a more inclusive attitude in someone who would have likely known about oppression.

Of course, the United States does not have a caste system per-se, yet, California has now deemed it necessary to outlaw caste as a means of discrimination.[26] California has some of the largest Indian communities in the world, which powers our high-tech companies. People continue to perpetrate abuses upon others because of a deemed "superiority" even in a nation seeking to create equality for all.

Why do people who have been oppressed feel a need to oppress others? Does a bully need to bully in order to heal their bully pain body? How can we heal past hurts before we hurt others? It is probably all in the shadow work Carl Jung spoke so much about. Of course, breaking the circle of separation, snobbery, and violence takes brave self-reflection, something not all people can or will do. The idea of superiority comes from a place of oppression. This should be self-evident, and all people should try to dismantle this.

I grew up with national pride about the United States. I wouldn't necessarily say I was nationalistic, but I believed our culture was positive with its inclusivity, especially since it was in our founding documents—then I learned about the three-fifths (3/5) compromise. The 3/5 compromise in the U.S. Constitution allowed slave states to

DON'T IDENTIFY WITH IT

count slaves as part of their population so those white states could have more representation in Congress (a slave was considered 3/5 of a person); you can read more about it on ChatGPT. This is why we must doubt everything we hear. How can we believe everyone is equal if we don't treat people of color as equal? I learned about the 3/5 clause in a matter-of-fact U.S. government class in middle school in the 1980s and my personal world fell apart. I felt betrayed by the America I once knew. (Of course, there were more betrayals to come from the historical establishment which once believed women to be property and had no right to vote—this was heartbreaking.) It wasn't until 1965 that no state could stop someone from voting based on ethnicity if they were a U.S. citizen.

Today, as tomorrow, the unenlightened powerful will attempt to shore up their world with exclusivity and ideas of *I'm more equal than you*. Watch those opinions, those sneaky dogmas that hide behind national pride, community building, and clubs. I always cringe when someone says, "I have to find my tribe." Still, though tribalism is another form of exclusivity, finding one's tribe can also be empowering—sometimes you need like-minded people with similar experiences in order to create change, especially if the group has been historically disempowered by power structures. Let's face facts: our power structures are based on a system of marginalizing "the other"—the power players "don't look like the ones who don't make the rules." Therefore, our potential is our saving grace. America grew from words that established our nation to be free from tyrants, religious dogma and, ultimately, gave us freedom to choose how we live:

> We hold these truths to be self-evident, that all men are created equal, that they are endowed by their Creator with certain unalienable Rights, that among these are Life, Liberty and the pursuit of Happiness.

–Opening line of the "Declaration of Independence," mostly attributed to Thomas Jefferson

Let's not be like Thomas Jefferson: an abolitionist and a slave owner.

Chapter 11
We Are All Criminally Insane

"Why are you quitting?" I asked this fresh-faced millennial. (Let's call her Tory as I can't remember her real name). "Tory, why are you quitting?" I asked again. I was pained. She was good at her job. I remember that because it's surprisingly hard to find good people in this job; I dislike losing them.

"I want to work with the criminally insane." Actually—she probably didn't say *that*, but my paraphrase is correct. Tory possessed a degree in psychology and had accepted a job at the federal prison—San Quentin—just north of San Francisco.

I work in the legal field.

I had this image of Tory, doing the pros and cons list side by side and deciding (with her hands outstretched like the scales held by the Goddess of Justice) which job to choose. The weight of being an immigration paralegal had her right hand hitting the floor, and working with the criminally insane had her left hand reaching for the stars. There you are... it is what it is and nothing more than that.

There are many reasons I believe we all have a little bit of "the criminal" in us and that more than half of us are more than a bit crazy. (I thought Tory was at least crazy to take a job in a federal prison.) In the blink of an eye, we can receive information from anywhere in the world; yet, just like in the old days, it is often urban myths and misinformation due to someone's agenda. We live in a world of absurdity: moving forward two steps from where we are and three steps backward to where someone else wants us to be. The result is a lateral movement of the post-modern backward angle.

The protagonist—resentful, angry, and a bit psychotic—must be peddling the dissemination of falsity and fear, right? However, I give pause, as this problem of angst, alienation, and psychosis spreads beyond the diagnosed criminally insane. With the technology available today, we all now hold this disruptive and destructive power (and a bit of madness). If a person possesses hell-bent anger with the world, and psychosis to boot, the ability to create mayhem on a microlevel exponentially becomes a macro problem.

We are all very close to being a bit off, if not sort of Hitler-like, and technology gives us all the power. We don't need an army to cause large-scale mayhem anymore.

I hope to provide some insight through this zig-zagging maze of strangeness; after all, if we are aware of our tendencies toward sociopathy, and know it, we can prevent it. Hence the purpose of the following stories. Maybe, with a bit of humorous reflection, we can all learn—or not, after all, learning anything is dependent on the person.

Life Is Too Short to Take Seriously, or COVID-19

"One of you go to the garage!" I bellow from upstairs. We are all home. "Shelter in Place" is the order from our local counties in Silicon Valley in response to COVID-19's rapid spread. It is taking a toll on family dynamics. My two teenage girls are learning remotely, but also giggling and screeching at each other. They both procure pillows and blankets and go into the garage. I am oblivious to a pubescent, clever interpretation of my order; after all, I didn't say *which one* should go to the insulated and decently warm garage. But now it is quiet, and I can work—remotely.

I wish I could tell you I don't care, but I do. I cannot be completely unaffected by all the fear and angst surrounding COVID-19. Laughing helps. Being a tad off helps. Most importantly, seeing humor in the macabre helps. Life is completely up to your perception—this scares people. However, in the case of the COVID-19 issue, it really is up to your age, which last time I checked, is sort of up to the linear timeline of reality.

Old people are getting hit hard.

As my kids would say: the "Boomers are being boomed." Right now, I am sequestered in my house, with my husband, two children, two cats and a feeling of "what now, son?" It's a bit surreal. Maybe the days of "Mad Max" are upon us. However, I enjoy working from home. California, being on the leading tech edge (tech gurus *love* to tell you everything is "cutting edge"), was able to adjust quickly to the remote work idea.

Even before the current state and federal administrations took action on COVID-19, high tech companies, in response to the pandemic, encouraged working from home. The companies also issued mandatory no-international travel to their employees before we were hit with more COVID-19 cases.

The Federal Government was slow to act (unless you are a Trump supporter, then they've done a "great" job and "America is GREAT again").

The company I work for provides an "essential" service and we are, at this time, ordered to shelter in place unless you provide an "essential" service. Apparently, legal services are essential. But in order to create social distancing to prevent the spread of COVID-19, my work team is rotating our presence in the office. This is not mandatory, but not optional either. (Yeah, *you* tell me what that means).

I like working from home because, in my solitude, I can think. Absurdity and contradictions abound when one pauses to think: *like, what if you don't have a shelter?* In Silicon Valley, we have a problem with homelessness, hence the Catch-22 of someone living outside and being required to stay in shelter (although California governor, Gavin Newsom, reflected on the "Shelter-in-Place" order by saying (paraphrased): "This order does not apply to the homeless.")

It's nice not to be homeless. I can shelter in place, have some tea, coffee, and a walk outside, as long as I stay six feet away from others. I have to say: solitude appeals to the hermit in me. I like myself, at least my thoughts. They make me laugh (if you haven't figured it out yet; I'm also a bit "off"). If you have an image of me walking around giggling to myself, it's all part of my plan for social distancing.

There is a downside to all this though. There has been a rush for toilet paper. And you have to wonder why. Apparently, you can live without food—there is still plenty of that around—but toilet paper—that's a hot commodity.

But then I thought about it...*what is someone to do without toilet paper??!!! I mean regular paper is gross. Can't flush that. You could take a shower after such messy stuff, I suppose.* Yes—I can feel the panic welling up. **I. Now. Need** 500 rolls of toilet paper before it's too late. *I better stock up!*

(Pause here for some online shopping.)

I'm back. I just went online to order delivery from our wholesale market. When I did a search for "toilet paper," the search engine came up with a 50-year-old French cognac. Actually, I stand corrected, it costs $50 and it's "XO Cognac" and the "XO" stands for "Extra Old," which means, according to online sources (not fake online sources), the Cognac is older than 20 years old. I put it in my virtual cart on a whim, thinking, *if I can't wipe myself clean, I can be "wiped clean" by over-priced alcohol and "wipe the floor clean" as I fall on my drunken face. It does sound like a grand scheme, so maybe there is no downside.*

My Co-Dependent Cats and Body Positivity

"Acccckkkkrrggg... ack...ack..." My male tuxedo cat, Bernard, is heaving and it makes me sad—less because I am sympathetic to his plight, as I know what is going to happen next. "Ack...ack..." He gives one last heave and throws up all over my carpet. Before I can stop my own gagging to clean it, my other cat, Clara, comes over to lick some up. She's an enabler.

I'm not sure if you are familiar with Laurel and Hardy, but they were the fat and skinny comedy duo from the early 20th century movies. My cat, Clara, my silver-grey tabby, is the fat one; Bernard is the skinny one. Bernard is bulimic and Clara is all about body positivity.

However, Clara doesn't understand how to stop Bernard's habit of gorging and purging. She enables his bulimic habit with her acceptance and encouragement of his behavior; although, practically speaking, the need to eat anything edible or partially digested likely comes from her feral history. (Bernard and Clara were both found in a vacant lot behind the veterans hospital near Stanford University.)

Bernard, who sits on anyone, often stretches his paw out and gives you a tap if he wants attention; whereas, Clara, a skittery, chubby, anxiety-filled cat will sit next to you and purr and self-soothe by rubbing her whisker-filled cheeks on your chair. She will then face-plant in the crook of your arm, but she will *not* sit on your lap. If you get close to her, without touching her, she will purr loudly, seemingly wanting attention. But, if you make a sudden movement, she will skedaddle, and you will hear the sharp tapping of nails as she runs and slides along the wooden hallway floor. At full speed, down the not-more-than-8-foot-long hallway, she usually slips two-thirds of the way, and you can hear her stop with a bump against a door with a softened "thwat." She *needs* her nine lives.

Maybe we all need nine lives to figure things out.

On Not Being a "Boomer"

"'K, Boomer" was my sixteen-year-old's response—well, to anything really. It's a disrespectful reference to my aging philosophy (and yes, I know it was a meme from Australia, with some historical and political references). It makes me laugh, ironically. There was a time when the mantra of the baby boomer was "Don't trust anyone over 30," so yes, things have come full circle.

"I'm not a boomer," I say forcefully, knowing she'll keep bringing it up because the term pushes my buttons. "I am Generation X." She's tuned out by now, doing some "tick-tock" or "Instagram post," or "follow," or whatever them youngins are doing these days.

I find the use of terms, such as "boomer," "Generation X,Y,Z," and now, "millennial," very interesting. They seem to all hate each other, too. In general, by their sheer mass, the boomers are the oldest generation on Earth, and according to their forefathers, who complained about them, the "baby boomers" never knew hardship like they had: Boomers had never known poverty (The Great Depression); or war (WWI; WWII); or seen a lynching (KKK)—they were self-involved, entitled, and selfish. Yet, the boomers knew Vietnam, the Great Recession (they lost much of their retirement during those years), and have been instrumental in the development of Medicare, civil rights, and ending the Vietnam war. Now, millennials are called self-involved, entitled, and selfish—mostly by boomers.

The beat goes on.

Ironically, most of the pigeon-holing of any generation has to do with economics. Marketing employs stereotyping boxes to understand a particular market, with generational themes, for a target audience to sell stuff nobody needs. There was a famous Pepsi advertisement in the 1970s that used a famous "hippie song" by the New Seekers, whose lyrics started: "I'd like to teach the world to sing in perfect harmony...," a perfect "boomer" song. That song is a good song and one we should all embrace instead of hating each other. The world is stressful enough without all this hate—to borrow millennial Taylor Swift's lyrics:

> Haters gonna hate, hate, hate, hate, hate...
> I'm just gonna shake, shake, shake, shake
> I shake it off, I shake it off...

Chapter 12
It's Not Kansas, but It's a Potential

Question dogma. Question the magic pill. Question the status quo. Our desire to be safe makes us complacent in a world of change. Be yourself, and do not be tied to what society says you should be like. I grew up with Generation X, who embraced punk, blue hair, and pierced cheeks—because we were angry. We were okay with the ever-changing color of the Emerald City because our beliefs were constantly being challenged. America had not kept its promise. Everywhere we looked there was hypocrisy. It smothered us with patriotism but wouldn't take care of veterans coming back from the Vietnam war. It told us not to lie, yet there was Clarence Thomas. It told us to work hard, yet the rents kept going up and the wages didn't. It gave everyone before my generation a free education, a job, a pension package, medical support, but left us behind to fend for ourselves. We were called "slackers and losers," yet the boomer generation labeling us was about "love and peace."

The civil rights movement had made gains, but it had a way to go on a societal level—the creation of a society that did not judge based on gender and race. Yet, "equality" was becoming more and more a possibility within the legal system.

Our society still told women to be a certain way: feminine; pretty; skinny; graceful; kind; stupid; smart; Ivy League; not too funny; etc. The labels remained but the legal structures around equality started to change in the 1950s to 1970s before the Reagan era, at which time the baby boomers and religious fanatics decided things had gone too far—basically because the evangelical capitalists were no longer getting enough butter for their bread.

Today, many in the boomer generation say they don't like being invisible because of their age. *WTF?* My *entire* generation was invisible. I have never had any problem being invisible. Being a cog in the machine—yes, that bugs me—but invisibility? NO. We had to get a job to survive. It became apparent that our society was about work. Our hierarchies of getting rich demanded that we strive to be a certain way. Even our religions were about work. I never found Jesus. I never found God in any of this (I found my soul), but when I said, "fuck it" and refused to identify with a specific way of being, I found freedom. I had to stop caring what other people thought, what society said, and look closely at my triggers and resolve issues when interacting with the world. I still think my soul expansion is a work in progress, and I am okay with not figuring everything out. If we embrace the idea that change is constant and good, and do not identify with what we want too much and who we are too much, and release attachment to those things, this will help us ameliorate self-suffering. We become souls who can experience and grow in the society around us.

Why did I write this book? Frankly, because I was tired of men mansplaining about my reality. Fundamentally, I do believe there is a source/energy amongst all of us, a soul consciousness that lives on. This energy is what helped me write this book. Some call it channeling. The more skeptical side of me does not believe I channeled anything but like-minded beliefs from other sources I have already read, aggregated, and sharpened ... words based on years and years of education and frustration with what had been presented to me as "truths."

I hope this book will help open your mind. Fundamentally, this is what we are here on earth for: to change, to grow our consciousness. Whereas evil vs. good are human constructs, a good feeling from helping others, being kind, and being inclusive lasts long after we are dead. We build on the ideals of humanity because we know, at a soul level, we should. We build on our inclusivity without a special agenda, except for the agenda of being human. Humans are frustrating at best, detrimental to everything at worst. With an eye for seeing things with an open mind, where sneaky belief systems don't trap us in perceptions that separate, divide, suppress, oppress, and confine—we can free our mind.

So, be loquaciously brave in your travels. Self-reflection cannot destroy your eternal soul, but it can make you uncomfortable. *Be uncomfortable.*

Listen to the drag queens. They have some words of wisdom...

"GREAT, THAT'S JUST WHAT THIS COUNTRY NEEDS: A COCK IN A FROCK ON A ROCK." –The Adventures of Priscilla, Queen of the Desert

About the Author

Like humanity, I am a work in progress.

Being naively inspired to be open to learning, I make mistakes.

I've changed my mind so many times, but I am okay with this.

[1] Buddhists, priests, monastics, and others on the spiritual path often practice detachment from the material and believe attachment, in any form, enslaves the mind.

[2] https://abc7news.com/teen-mental-health-statistics-cdc-covid-resources-awareness/11697913/

[3] "Buddha's words would create silence because Buddha is the *manifestation* of silence. Silence is the source of life and is the cure for diseases. When people are angry, they maintain silence. First they shout and then silence dawns." https://wisdom.srisriravishankar.org/buddha-is-the-manifestation-of-silence/#:~:text=Buddha's%20words%20would%20definitely%20create,shout%20and%20th[1]

[4] "Scripture tells us that silence can help us avoid sinning (Proverbs 10:19), gain respect (Proverbs 11:12), and is deemed wise and intelligent (Proverbs 17:28). In other words, you may be blessed by holding your tongue." https://openthebible.org/article/knowing-when-to-speak-and-when-to-be-silent/#:~:text=Scripture%20tells%20us%20that%20silence,we%20are%20practicing%20self[2]

[5] Ibid., "Ultimately, refraining from speaking in certain situations means we are practicing self-control."

[6] Buddhist Society of Western Australia. "Non-Self - a Unique Teaching of the Buddha | Ajahn Brahmali | 21-11-2014," November 23, 2014. https://www.youtube.com/watch?v=QVQpdbAWSS8.

---

1. https://wisdom.srisriravishankar.org/buddha-is-the-manifestation-of-silence/#_853ae90f0351324bd73ea615e6487517__4c761f170e016836ff84498202b99827__853ae90f0351324bd73ea615e6487517_text_43ec3e5dee6e706af7766fffea512721_Buddha_3590cb8af0bbb9e78c343b52b93773c9_s_0bcef9c45bd8a48eda1b26eb0c61c869_20words_0bcef9c45bd8a48eda1b26eb0c61c869_20would_0bcef9c45bd8a48eda1b26eb0c61c869_20definitely_0bcef9c45bd8a48eda1b26eb0c61c869_20create_c0cb5f0fcf239ab3d9c1fcd31fff1efc_shout_0bcef9c45bd8a48eda1b26eb0c61c869_20and_0bcef9c45bd8a48eda1b26eb0c61c869_20then_0bcef9c45bd8a48eda1b26eb0c61c869_20silence_0bcef9c45bd8a48eda1b26eb0c61c869_20dawns

2. https://openthebible.org/article/knowing-when-to-speak-and-when-to-be-silent/#_853ae90f0351324bd73ea615e6487517__4c761f170e016836ff84498202b99827__853ae90f0351324bd73ea615e6487517_text_43ec3e5dee6e706af7766fffea512721_Scripture_0bcef9c45bd8a48eda1b26eb0c61c869_20tells_0bcef9c45bd8a48eda1b26eb0c61c869_20us_0bcef9c45bd8a48eda1b26eb0c61c869_20that_0bcef9c45bd8a48eda1b26eb0c61c869_20silence_c0cb5f0fcf239ab3d9c1fcd31fff1efc_we_0bcef9c45bd8a48eda1b26eb0c61c869_20are_0bcef9c45bd8a48eda1b26eb0c61c869_20practicing_0bcef9c45bd8a48eda1b26eb0c61c869_20self_0bcef9c45bd8a48eda1b26eb0c61c869_2Dcontrol

[7] Gordon-Roth, Jessica, "Locke on Personal Identity", The Stanford Encyclopedia of Philosophy (Spring 2020 Edition), Edward N. Zalta (ed.), URL = <https://plato.stanford.edu/archives/spr2020/entries/locke-personal-identity/>.

[8] Morris, William Edward and Charlotte R. Brown, "David Hume", The Stanford Encyclopedia of Philosophy (Summer 2022 Edition), Edward N. Zalta (ed.), URL = <https://plato.stanford.edu/archives/sum2022/entries/hume/>.

[9] OSHO Times. "This Is Why Osho Called Mother Teresa a 'Deceiver', 'Charlatan' and 'Hypocrite.'" *HuffPost*, HuffPost, 21 Sept. 2016, https://www.huffpost.com/archive/in/entry/this-is-why-osho-called-mother-teresa-a-deceiver-charlatan_a_21472508.

[10] Leaf, C.E. *Switch on Your Brain + Switch on Your Brain Workbook + Switch on Your Brain DVD: The Key to ... Peak Happiness, Thinking, and Health, Curriculum K.*, Baker Book House, 2018.

[11] Aristotle saw a specific separation of slaves and non-slaves. Yet, the questioning of social norms by the ancients that meant the "justification" of slaves and women being "separate'" could be questioned and ultimately challenged as being illogical.

[12] Cates, Diana Fritz. "Conceiving Emotions: Martha Nussbaum's Upheavals of Thought." *Journal of Religious Ethics*, vol. 31, no. 2, June 2003, pp. 325–341, doi:10.1111/1467-9795.00140.

[13] https://www.washingtonpost.com/dc-md-va/2022/07/30/body-shame-win-teenager-gaetz/

[14] https://www.youtube.com/watch?v=ntrnhNmOLIE

[15] Benatar, David. "Better Never to Have Been: The Harm of Coming into Existence." *OUP Academic*, Oxford University Press, 12 Oct. 2006, academic.oup.com/book/32901. Accessed 03 June 2023.

[16] https://www.nbcnews.com/video/man-intentionally-drove-tesla-off-cliff-with-family-inside-wife-says-174839877835

[17] https://en.wikipedia.org/wiki/Luna_(tree)

[18] https://www.endocrineweb.com/news/problems-with-BMI

[19] https://www.sciencedirect.com/science/article/abs/pii/S0376871621006773#:~:text=On%20the%20other%20hand%2C%20less,et%20al.%2C%20(

[20] https://psychnews.psychiatryonline.org/doi/full/10.1176/appi.pn.2020.8a16

[21] https://www.tutorhunt.com/resource/22936/#:~:text=In%20this%20line%20of%20thought,disorder%20(Freud%2C%201901)

[22] https://psychnews.psychiatryonline.org/doi/full/10.1176/appi.pn.2020.8a16

[23] https://www.scientificamerican.com/article/do-we-live-in-a-simulation-chances-are-about-50-50/

[24] "The caste system is a social structure that has its roots in ancient India. It is a hierarchical system of social stratification based on birth, occupation, and hereditary distinctions. The caste system divides society into distinct groups known as castes, with each caste having a prescribed set of rights, privileges, and obligations." [Pulled from ChatGPT]

[25] https://www.pewresearch.org/religion/2021/06/29/attitudes-about-caste/

[26] https://www.nbcnews.com/news/asian-america/california-one-step-closer-banning-caste-based-discrimination-rcna81555

---

3. https://www.sciencedirect.com/science/article/abs/pii/S0376871621006773#_853ae90f0351324bd73ea615e6487517__4c761f170e016836ff84498202b99827__853ae90f0351324bd73ea615e6487517_text_43ec3e5dee6e706af7766fffea512721_On_0bcef9c45bd8a48eda1b26eb0c61c869_20the_0bcef9c45bd8a48eda1b26eb0c61c869_20other_0bcef9c45bd8a48eda1b26eb0c61c869_20hand_0bcef9c45bd8a48eda1b26eb0c61c869_2C_0bcef9c45bd8a48eda1b26eb0c61c869_20less_c0cb5f0fcf239ab3d9c1fcd31fff1efc_et_0bcef9c45bd8a48eda1b26eb0c61c869_20al._0bcef9c45bd8a48eda1b26eb0c61c869_2C_0bcef9c45bd8a48eda1b26eb0c61c869_202008

4. https://www.tutorhunt.com/resource/22936/#_853ae90f0351324bd73ea615e6487517__4c761f170e016836ff84498202b99827__853ae90f0351324bd73ea615e6487517_text_43ec3e5dee6e706af7766fffea512721_In_0bcef9c45bd8a48eda1b26eb0c61c869_20this_0bcef9c45bd8a48eda1b26eb0c61c869_20line_0bcef9c45bd8a48eda1b26eb0c61c869_20of_0bcef9c45bd8a48eda1b26eb0c61c869_20thought_c0cb5f0fcf239ab3d9c1fcd31fff1efc_disorder_0bcef9c45bd8a48eda1b26eb0c61c869_20_84c40473414caf2ed4a7b1283e48bbf4_Freud_0bcef9c45bd8a48eda1b26eb0c61c869_2C_0bcef9c45bd8a48eda1b26eb0c61c869_201901_9371d7a2e3ae86a00aab4771e39d255d_

www.ingramcontent.com/pod-product-compliance
Lightning Source LLC
Chambersburg PA
CBHW031650040426
42453CB00006B/261